THANK GOD
for this
AMAZING MAN

A 45 Day Devotional and Journal

EBONY N. MAYO

NOTE

Presented to: _____

By: _____

Date: _____

Thank God for this Amazing Man
A 45-Day Prayer Devotional and Journal

Published by JM Publishing LLC
New York, NY, U.S.A.
www.jmpublishingllc.com

Book Cover Design by Anže Ban Virant – ABV Atelier Design

Library of Congress Cataloging-in-Publication Data is available upon request

Quantity Purchases:

Churches, men's ministries, schools, organizations, and other groups may qualify for special terms when ordering quantities of this title. For more information, please email info@ebonynmayo.com or visit www.ebonynmayo.com

This book is printed in the United States of America.

GRATITUDE

To my parents, **Sylvester Mayo Sr. and Arlene Mayo** — thank you for your unwavering love and support since the moment you brought me into this world. I honor God for the gift of you.

To my **brothers, aunts, uncles, my late great-grandmother Janie Carter, my godmother, god-sister, family, friends and spiritual leaders** — each of you has planted seeds of wisdom, faith, and love in different seasons of my life. Your presence has been a continuous blessing, and I am deeply grateful.

To **all of the men** who have followed and connected with my social media prayers — thank you for allowing my words to meet you where you are. My light honors your light.

And lastly, but never least, to **God**, the source of it all — my deepest gratitude for your grace, favor, and endless love. All praise and glory to You, forever.

CONTENTS

INTRODUCTION

Men Need Love, Too and They Need a Fight Plan

We live in a world that constantly tells men to "man up," "stay strong," and "handle it." But no one tells you how. No one tells you how to carry the weight of fatherhood, manhood, leadership, work, money, relationships, trauma, grief, loss, fear, doubt, and faith all at the same time without breaking.

The truth is you were never meant to carry it all alone.

You were created by God to be a leader, a protector, a builder, and a warrior. But even warriors need armor. Even kings need rest. Even the strongest men need spaces where they can lay it all down without shame or fear of judgment.

That is why this devotional exists. I created it with you in mind to give you what many men never hear, but desperately need: **You are seen. You are loved. You are appreciated. You are supported. You are Powerful.** Those are not just empty words, they are a declaration over your life, every day you open this book.

This 45 day journey is not about making you more religious or perfect. It is about inviting you into a sacred rhythm of healing, stillness, and rejuvenation, one that gives you permission to pause, reset, and let God meet you in the realest parts of your life.

Each day you will receive six powerful tools for your spirit, mind, and soul:

Reflection Question

A challenge to help you go deeper, confront your truth, and grow from the inside out.

Bold Prayer

Honest, raw, and real. Speaking directly to where you are as a man.

Scripture Anchor

A powerful verse to root you in the Word of God and remind you of His promises.

Daily Challenge

A prompt to help you move forward, take action, and rise when life feels heavy.

Daily Reminder Quote

A quote spoken by me, Ebony N. Mayo, to carry with you each day. These words were written exclusively for this journey.

Space to Release

A place to journal your thoughts, emotions, breakthroughs, and prayers.

You can walk through this devotional in two ways:

- One day at a time, following the journey in order, building a rhythm of connection and growth

OR

- When life feels heavy, through stress, grief, temptation, loss, depression, doubt, fatherhood, or whatever you are facing, you can turn directly to the day you need most. It's all here.

This is not just a devotional. **It is a fight plan** a spiritual training ground to prepare you for battle, to heal from the battles you have already fought, and to remind you of who you really are: A beloved son. A powerful man. A rising king.

Men are facing record breaking levels of stress, anxiety, loneliness, and depression, yet many still suffer in silence. It is time to break that silence.

This is your space. This is your permission. This is your restoration.

So take a deep breath. Lay it all down. And let us walk this journey together. Not for perfection, but for presence.

Show up for yourself. Show up for your purpose. Show up for your family. Show up for your God.

Man of God you are needed. You are chosen. You are worthy of rest, reflection, and renewal.

This is your fight plan. This is your time to rise.

Shalom

STRENGTH

(Endurance for the Journey, Power for the Fight)

Reflection Question:

Where in your life do you feel like you are running on empty? Where do you need a fresh infusion of strength?

DEAR GOD, THANK YOU FOR THIS AMAZING MAN:

God, I lift up this man to You right now the man reading these words, the man fighting silent battles nobody sees.

God, I know that You will not put more on him than he can bear, but in all honesty, this journey can feel unbearable at times. Even though he is not weak, this journey has been knocking the wind out of him. I pray that You will give him strength for the journey. Help him to endure this season as a good soldier. I speak strength to his strength.

When the pressures of life feel overwhelming on his shoulders, hold up his arms. Remind him he is not alone and that he has an army of angels at his disposal to help him when he feels weak.

God, You know the weight he carries. You know the nights he lies awake, replaying worries in his mind. You know the days when his shoulders ache not just from physical work, but from the emotional burden of providing, leading, and holding it all together. You see the moments when he smiles on the outside but feels worn thin inside. You see his silent prayers, his unshed tears, his quiet *"God, help me"* whispers.

Today, God, I pray You breathe fresh strength into his spirit. Like a warrior before battle, armor him up. Like a runner on the final lap, breathe fresh wind into his lungs. Like David facing Goliath, remind him that with You, he is unstoppable.

Just like in weightlifting, God You be his spotter when the weights are too heavy. Be his refuge when his mind grows weary. Be his shield when life attacks feel relentless. Surround him with brothers, mentors, and safe people who will lift his arms when they fall.

Let today be the day he rises again stronger, braver, and more grounded in You. Thank You, God, that You are his unshakable strength. Amen.

Scripture Reading:

"I can do all things through Christ who strengthens me." — Philippians 4:13 (NKJV)

Today's Challenge:

Write down one area where you feel drained or tired. Pray: *"God, I surrender this to You today. Be my strength."* Watch how God shows up.

Daily Reminder Quote:

"There is a fire inside you the world has not seen yet. You are stronger than every fear, every failure, and every storm because God's strength lives in you." — *Ebony N. Mayo*

Journal Space:

(What areas of your life are testing your strength right now? Be honest about where you feel stretched and where you are ready to grow stronger.)

_____

_____

_____

_____

_____

_____

_____

_____

_____

_____

_____

_____

_____

PURPOSE

(Walking Boldly in Divine Assignment)

Reflection Question:

Have you truly discovered your God-given purpose? Are you actively pursuing it, or have you been drifting, distracted, or doubting?

DEAR GOD, THANK YOU FOR THIS AMAZING MAN:

God, I thank You for this man's life for the fact that before he was even born, You wrote a purpose over him, a purpose bigger than a paycheck, bigger than titles, bigger than the world's expectations.

But God, sometimes, he wonders if he has missed it. Sometimes, the noise of life drowns out Your voice. Sometimes, family pressures, societal demands, and his own self-doubt make him question if he will ever become the man You have called him to be.

Today, God, I pray You ignite something fresh inside him. Help him to discover his true purpose and identity not defined by what others say, but grounded in You. I rebuke every word curse ever spoken over him, every lie that told him he would never amount to anything, every seed of negativity planted in his heart. Right now, God, I pull those lies up by the roots so they will not grow. Instead, I plant seeds of purpose, clarity, certainty, identity, and power.

Remind him he is important. He is needed. He is desired. Remind him that his purpose is not random, it is specific, intentional, and tailor-made. He is the only one who can carry out the mission You have assigned to him.

God, I pray You awaken the gifts and passions You placed inside him. Help him move from surviving to thriving.

Combine his purpose with his passion so that his life blesses not only himself, but everyone he touches. Wherever he has settled, light a holy fire. Wherever he has drifted, bring him back. Wherever he feels lost, be his guide and compass.

Surround him with people who speak life over him, who call out the gold in him, who remind him of his calling when he forgets. Thank You, God, for making the world a better place by creating this man. Thank You that his purpose is wrapped in Your will and You will bring it to pass.
Amen.

Scripture Reading:

"Many are the plans in a person's heart, but it is the Lord's purpose that prevails." — Proverbs 19:21 (NIV)

Today's Challenge:

Write down ONE passion or gift you have. Pray: *"God, show me how You want me to use this for Your glory."* Take one small step today to activate that purpose.

Daily Reminder Quote:

"You were created on purpose, for a purpose and no one else can carry the assignment God placed on your life." — *Ebony N. Mayo*

Journal Space:

(What is one dream, idea, or gift that keeps tugging at your heart? Write it out even if it feels far away. Purpose begins with awareness.)

_____

_____

_____

_____

_____

_____

_____

_____

_____

_____

_____

_____

_____

FAMILY

(Covering Loved Ones With Love and Prayer)

Reflection Question:

How can you show up better for your family today? If you are preparing for a family, how can you begin laying the foundation now?

DEAR GOD, THANK YOU FOR THIS AMAZING MAN:

*G*od, I lift up this man and his family to You. You know his heart and his deep desire to love, protect, and lead his family well. But God, family dynamics are not always simple.

We do not get to choose the family we are born into, and sometimes, we do not even have the final say in the families we create. There are wounds, unspoken hurts, and complex dynamics that only You can heal. Please touch his family. Heal the broken places, the silent gaps, and the strained relationships. Keep his family safe and his family circle unbroken. Draw them closer together, shaping them into a healthy, loving, and supportive unit.

God, help those who have gone astray and bring back those who have become estranged. Where there is distance, bring connection. Where there is bitterness, bring forgiveness. Where there is silence, bring conversation.

If he has children, God, cover them. Keep them safe, healthy, respectful, loving, joyful, and blessed. Help him to parent with wisdom, grace, and patience, even in tough situations like co-parenting or blended families. Let his relationship with his partner blossom for the sake of a strong, unified family.

If he longs for children, I bind infertility and every obstacle in his way. Bless him with the gift of fatherhood. Remind him that his family, whether by blood or by choice, is one of the greatest treasures You have given him.

Help him to show up not just as a provider of money, but as a provider of presence, time, love, and emotional connection. Give him humility to apologize when needed, strength to lead when it is hard, and grace to cover his family with peace.

Thank You, God, for the beautiful gift of family. Thank You for the role this man plays in shaping a legacy of love that will ripple for generations.
Amen.

Scripture Reading:

"How good and pleasant it is when God's people live together in unity!" — Psalm 133:1 (NIV)

Today's Challenge:

Do ONE intentional act of love today for your family. Whether it is a call, a hug, a text, a prayer, or simply being present, take one step to show up fully.

Daily Reminder Quote:

"No family is perfect, but family is what you make it and how you show up can change everything." — *Ebony N. Mayo*

Journal Space:

(What does your family mean to you? What relationships need healing, attention, or gratitude? Write out the weight and the love you carry.)

_____

_____

_____

_____

_____

_____

_____

_____

_____

_____

_____

_____

FAITH

(Believing Without Limits)

Reflection Question:

What do you need faith for right now? Where are you struggling to believe, and where do you need to trust God more deeply?

DEAR GOD, THANK YOU FOR THIS AMAZING MAN:

*G*od, I lift up this man's faith today, the faith that has been tested, stretched, and sometimes shaken.

You said in Your Word that even faith the size of a mustard seed can move mountains. So today, God, I pray You stir up mustard-seed faith inside him.

Give him bold, wild, childlike faith, the kind of faith that dreams big without worrying about the "how." Help him to stop overthinking and overanalyzing, and instead, remind him to simply believe.

Remind him that he walks by faith, not by sight. You know where his faith has been under attack: the disappointments, the delays, the detours that made him wonder if You still hear him. Maybe he has been believing for something, a breakthrough, a miracle, a new chapter and it has not come yet.

But God, renew his faith today. Infuse him with trust, patience, and holy expectation. Surround him with people who have big faith, people who will fuel his belief, not drain it.

Help him to believe You for the "big ask" the dreams that seem impossible, the doors that look closed. Remind him that nothing is too hard for You, and nothing is beyond Your reach.

Thank You that his faith is not just for blessings but for battles. Faith is what strengthens him when storms come. Faith is what carries him when the road is long. Faith is what pleases You, God and today, I pray You multiply it in his life.

Through faith, let him see miracles, signs, wonders, and victories that no one can explain except by Your power. Thank You, God, for being faithful even when he struggles to believe.
Amen.

Scripture Reading:

"For we walk by faith, not by sight." — 2 Corinthians 5:7 (NKJV)

Today's Challenge:

Write down ONE thing you have been afraid to ask God, something big. Pray: "God, I believe You can do this. Help my unbelief." Take one small faith step today toward that prayer.

Daily Reminder Quote:

"Faith is not about seeing the whole picture, it is about trusting the One who holds the brush." — Ebony N. Mayo

Journal Space:

(Where is your faith today strong, shaken, or searching? Write honestly to God about what you are trusting Him for or what you need help believing again.)

_____

_____

_____

_____

_____

_____

_____

_____

_____

_____

_____

_____

CAREER

(Excellence, Integrity, and Increase in Work)

Reflection Question:

Are you thriving in your career or just surviving? Does your work align with your purpose and passion, or has it become just a paycheck?

DEAR GOD, THANK YOU FOR THIS AMAZING MAN:

God, today I lift up this man's career before You.

You see his daily grind: the early mornings, the late nights, the pressure to perform, provide, and succeed. You see when he feels fulfilled, and You see when he feels stuck, overlooked, or restless. You know the quiet fears he carries about money, stability, purpose, and whether his work really matters.

God, I pray You breathe fresh vision into his career. Help him to not just clock in and survive, but to thrive. Help him to wake up excited about the work You have given him, to see his job not just as a paycheck, but as a platform for purpose.

Where there is stagnation, open new doors. Where there is frustration, give him wisdom and strategy. Where there is discouragement, remind him of his worth. Surround him with colleagues, clients, supervisors, and partners who respect him. Help him to respect himself enough to walk away from environments that no longer serve his growth.

God, I ask for promotions, opportunities, unexpected favor, and increase. Let his name carry weight in rooms he has not even entered yet. Let him be seen not just as a worker, but as a man of integrity, creativity, and excellence.

And Lord, keep him covered as he works. Protect his life while he provides for his family especially if his work is dangerous, labor-intensive, or puts him at risk. Shield him from accidents, injuries, and harm. Let him make it home safely every day to those who love and need him.

Remind him, God, that his identity is not tied to a title or a paycheck. He is not just his job he is Your son, called, chosen, and anointed for greatness both inside and outside of his career. Thank You for blessing the work of his hands, for multiplying his efforts, and for opening doors no man can shut.
Amen.

Scripture Reading:

"Commit your work to the Lord, and your plans will be established."
— Proverbs 16:3 (ESV)

Today's Challenge:

Identify ONE area of your career where you have been coasting or feeling stuck. Pray: "God, give me a fresh strategy and open doors in this area." Take one small action today even if it is just writing down a new idea.

Daily Reminder Quote:

"You are not defined by your job title, you are defined by God." — Ebony N. Mayo

Journal Space:

(Are you fulfilled in your current work or feeling stuck, overlooked, or overworked? Write about what you are building, dreaming of, or praying for in your career.)

_____

_____

_____

_____

_____

_____

_____

_____

_____

_____

_____

_____

VISION

(Clarity for the Future, Focus for Today)

Reflection Question:

When was the last time you wrote out your vision and made it plain? Do you know where you are headed, or are you moving through life without a target?

DEAR GOD, THANK YOU FOR THIS AMAZING MAN:

God, today I pray for this man's vision not just what he sees with his natural eyes, but what You have placed in his spirit.

Your Word says, "Where there is no vision, the people perish." He was never meant to just drift through life, settling for survival. He is called to build, to lead, and to thrive with purpose.

So, God, sharpen his vision. Remove the fog. Silence the noise. Interrupt the confusion.

If he has been coasting or distracted, let this be the day his sight becomes clear again. Give him 20/20 spiritual vision not only for one area of his life, but for every part: spiritually, emotionally, financially, mentally, physically, and relationally. Align his entire being so that nothing is out of order.

Stretch his vision, God. Do not let him think small. Let his vision extend to legacy, impact, and generations yet to come. Reveal the blueprint. Show him the playbook. Give him the courage to write it down and run with it.

And when the vision feels overwhelming, remind him he does not have to do it alone. Send mentors, partners, provision, and strategy to help him carry it. Surround him with the right people who will build with him, not distract him.

Most of all, remind him: he was made for this. He was created to see beyond the present and build for the future. Thank You, God, for giving him a vision rooted in Your will, a vision that elevates his life and blesses everyone connected to him.
Amen.

Scripture Reading:

"Write the vision and make it plain on tablets, that he may run who reads it." — Habakkuk 2:2 (NKJV)

Today's Challenge:

Take 10 minutes today to write out your vision even if it is not perfect. Pray: "God, sharpen my vision. Let me see clearly what You want me to build."

Daily Reminder Quote:

"Clarity is not just a gift, it is a weapon. Write your vision, run with it, and refuse to settle for less." — Ebony N. Mayo

Journal Space:

(Write out the vision you see for your life. Be bold. Be specific. Let it stretch beyond just today.)

_____

_____

_____

_____

_____

_____

_____

_____

_____

_____

_____

_____

_____

_____

INTRAPERSONAL RELATIONSHIP

(The Relationship You Have With Yourself)

Reflection Question:

Are you too hard on yourself? When was the last time you said something kind to yourself, out loud?

DEAR GOD, THANK YOU FOR THIS AMAZING MAN:

God, today I pray for this man's relationship with himself. You know the internal battles he has fought, the negative self-talk, the quiet shame, the expectations he carries that no one else sees.

God, he has been strong for others, shown grace to everyone else but struggled to show grace to himself. Help him today to see himself the way You see him. Not through the lens of past failures or mistakes, but through the lens of redemption, growth, and purpose.

God, teach him how to love himself, truly. Not in arrogance, but in awareness knowing he is worthy of love, worthy of peace, worthy of support. Worthy of healing. Worthy of progress. Help him to confront the parts of himself he has avoided, the shadows he has ignored, and the pain he has buried. Not to be ashamed but to be healed.

I come against every lie that has made him feel like he is not good enough. I bind the voice of the enemy that keeps replaying old wounds and false identities. Instead, I speak life. I speak renewal. I speak power and worth.

God, help him to forgive himself for what he did when he did not know better, and for who he had to be to survive. Show him how to clap for himself. To honor his growth. To speak to himself like he would to a friend. Remind him that he is not defined by his worst moments, but by the man he is becoming day by day, step by step.

Let every dormant gift in him rise again. Let every suppressed dream come back to life. Let him know *deep down* that he is still called, still chosen, and still capable of becoming everything You created him to be. Amen.

Scripture Reading:

"Therefore, if anyone is in Christ, he is a new creation. The old has passed away; behold, the new has come." — 2 Corinthians 5:17 (ESV)

Today's Challenge:

Look in the mirror and speak life over yourself. Say out loud: *"I am worthy. I am loved. I am becoming everything God created me to be."* Write down three things you love or respect about yourself.

Daily Reminder Quote:

"You pour into others. Just do not forget to pour into you. You are worthy of the love, grace, and patience you give away." — *Ebony N. Mayo*

Journal Space:

(What do you need to forgive yourself for? Write a letter to yourself, one full of grace, encouragement, and love. Remind yourself that you are still worthy, still becoming, and still chosen.)

_____

_____

_____

_____

_____

_____

_____

_____

_____

_____

_____

_____

_____

INTERPERSONAL RELATIONSHIPS

(How You Relate to Others)

Reflection Question:

Which relationship(s) in your life need more grace, honesty, or healing? Are there any that need boundaries or need to end?

DEAR GOD, THANK YOU FOR THIS AMAZING MAN:

*G*od, today I lift up the relationships in this man's life, every connection, from his closest circle to those he interacts with in passing. Each relationship has the power to build him up or break him down, so I pray You cover them all.

Teach him how to show up with love, integrity, and wisdom. Help him be a man who leads with honor, listens with compassion, and communicates with clarity. Give him the grace to forgive where it is needed and the courage to speak truth where silence has caused distance.

God, also give him discernment. Show him which relationships are meant to grow and which ones have reached their expiration date. If there are connections draining him, using him, or stunting his growth, give him the strength to release them without guilt. If there are relationships worth fighting for, equip him with patience, humility, and grace to rebuild them stronger.

Be the center of every bond in his life, romantic, family, friendships, business, and community. Where there is tension, bring peace. Where there is confusion, bring clarity. Where there is old wounds, bring healing.

Surround him with people who see his value beyond his hustle. Place true friends in his life who sharpen him, mentors who guide him, a partner who affirms him, and colleagues who respect him. Protect him from counterfeit connections and remind him he deserves relationships that are life-giving, not life-draining.

And if he has been walking alone, soften his heart to trust again. Break down the walls he built out of survival and let him know it is safe to be seen, safe to be supported, and safe to be loved.

God, align his relationships with the man You are calling him to be. Let every connection reflect truth, love, and growth.
Amen.

Scripture Reading:

"May the God who gives endurance and encouragement give you the same attitude of mind toward each other that Christ Jesus had." — Romans 15:5 (NLT)

Today's Challenge:

Identify one relationship that needs healing, clarity, or closure. Pray: "God, show me my role in this relationship." Then take one intentional step toward peace today.

Daily Reminder Quote:

"Some relationships need more grace. Others need more space. Knowing the difference will protect your peace." — *Ebony N. Mayo*

Journal Space:

(Write about the relationships in your life: the ones that fuel you, the ones that drain you, and the ones that may need forgiveness or release.)

_____

_____

_____

_____

_____

_____

_____

_____

_____

_____

_____

_____

LOVE

(The Power to Receive and Give)

Reflection Question:

Is love present in your life right now in a healthy, genuine way? Do you feel deeply loved, or are there wounds that still make it hard to receive love?

DEAR GOD, THANK YOU FOR THIS AMAZING MAN:

God, I thank You for this man, not just for what he does, but for who he is. Today, I pray he experiences real love. Not the shallow kind that comes and goes, not the kind tied to conditions, performance, or appearances but deep, steady, soul-healing love.

If he is in a relationship, God, cover it. Breathe life back into it where it feels dry. Reignite what has been lost. Take them back to the friendship, the laughter, the trust, and the connection that first brought them together. Let their love be built on truth, safety, faith, and respect.

If he is single, God, prepare him not just to find love, but to *receive* it without fear, hesitation, or doubt. Remind him that he is worthy of being loved for who he is, not for what he has or what he can do. Break down the walls that old wounds and disappointments have built around his heart. Heal the places where love once felt like pain, abandonment, or betrayal.

God, help him to forgive, to forgive those who did not know how to love him, and to forgive himself for the times he did not know how to love well. Do not let bitterness, skepticism, or shame close him off from what You are trying to give. Keep his heart soft, open, and ready.

Remind him today that You *are* love. And because he was made in Your image, love is already inside him. Show him that love is not weakness, it is power. That real love protects, uplifts, heals, and builds. Let him experience love that brings peace instead of chaos, clarity instead of confusion, joy instead of fear.

Whisper to his spirit today: "You are loved. You are worthy. You are seen. You are chosen not because of what you do, but because of who you are." Amen.

Scripture Reading:

"Love is patient, love is kind. It does not envy, it does not boast, it is not proud. It does not dishonor others, it is not self-seeking, it is not easily angered, it keeps no record of wrongs. Love does not delight in evil but rejoices with the truth. It always protects, always trusts, always hopes, always perseveres." — 1 Corinthians 13:4–7 (NIV)

Today's Challenge:

Write down the kind of love you want to give and the kind of love you want to receive. Pray: *"God, open my heart to give and receive love in the healthiest way."*

Daily Reminder Quote:

"Men deserve love too. Real love does not demand perfection, it simply requires presence. You are worthy of both: giving it and receiving it." — Ebony N. Mayo

Journal Space:

(Write honestly about your experiences with love, the good, the painful, and the areas that still need healing.)

_____

_____

_____

_____

_____

_____

_____

_____

_____

_____

_____

_____

_____

SAFE SPACES

(Where You Can Be Real Without Judgment and Offer the Same to Others)

Reflection Question:

Do you have a safe space, a person or a place where you can be fully honest, without fear or judgment? Do you believe your thoughts, emotions, and voice truly matter?

DEAR GOD, THANK YOU FOR THIS AMAZING MAN:

God, I lift up this man's heart today. You know the world he has had to navigate with a guarded soul. You know the pressure he has felt to always keep it together. You know the smile he has worn when his mind has been battling storms.

God, I pray You lead him to safe spaces, places and people where he does not have to pretend, perform, or protect. Spaces where he can exhale. Where he can let his guard down. Where he can speak freely. Cry if he needs to. Be seen. Be known. Be held up.

Remind him that vulnerability is not weakness, it is courage. Remind him that being in tune with his emotions does not make him soft, it makes him wise, grounded, and free.

God, protect him from environments where honesty is turned into a weapon. Surround him with people who do not just hear him, but understand him. People who do not just tolerate him, but value him. People who would not just keep him safe but empower him to rise higher.

Teach him how to create his own safe space, too. Let prayer be his sanctuary. Let solitude be his strength. Let brotherhood be his backup.

Give him discernment so he knows who deserves his trust. Do not let him lay his head in Delilah's lap in places of false comfort that drain his strength. Guard him from counterfeit connections, and surround him with men and women who will sharpen him, cover him, and protect what is sacred.

But God, also shape him into a safe space for others. Let his children know they can come to him without fear. Let his partner feel secure in his presence, covered in love and trust. Let his brothers and friends know they have someone who listens, uplifts, and protects without judgment. Make him the kind of man whose words heal instead of harm, whose presence gives peace instead of pressure.

And if he has been doing life alone for too long, give him the courage to ask for help. To speak up. To open up. To step into the spaces that heal instead of harm.

God, let him know today: he matters. His voice matters. His story matters. He deserves to have spaces that feel like home and he is also called to *be* that space for those he loves.
Amen.

Scripture Reading:

"The Lord is a refuge for the oppressed, a stronghold in times of trouble." — Psalm 9:9 (NIV) "I will say of the Lord, 'He is my refuge and my fortress, my God, in whom I trust.'" — Psalm 91:2 (NIV)

Today's Challenge:

Reach out to someone you trust and start a real conversation. Or pray: *"God, reveal and surround me with safe spaces where I can grow, heal, and be myself. And help me to become that safe space for the people You have placed in my life."*

Daily Reminder Quote:

"A real man does not just fight battles, he finds spaces to rest, reset, and heal. And he becomes that safe space for the ones he loves." — Ebony N. Mayo

Journal Space:

(Write about how safe or unsafe you have felt lately. What would a true safe space look like for you? How can you also become a safe space for others?)

_____

_____

_____

_____

_____

_____

_____

_____

_____

_____

_____

_____

HEALING

(The Process of Becoming Whole Again)

Reflection Question:

Are you or someone you love in need of healing physically, mentally, emotionally, spiritually, or financially? What areas have been hurting silently?

DEAR GOD, THANK YOU FOR THIS AMAZING MAN:

*G*od, today I pray for this man's healing not just on the surface, but deep in the hidden places where pain has lived too long. Heal the wounds no one else can see: the childhood trauma he buried, the broken relationships he carries like scars, the silent battles he never told a soul about.

If there is sickness in his body, I declare healing in the mighty name of Jesus. You are Jehovah-Rapha, the God who heals, and healing is not just what You do it is who You are. If he has been avoiding doctor's visits out of fear, give him courage to face the truth and meet him there with miracles. If someone he loves is battling illness, be the ultimate physician. Do what medicine cannot do. Speak peace to his heart and strength to their body.

But God, I know true healing goes far beyond what can be measured in the body. Heal his spirit where disappointment made him question You. Heal his mind where anxiety, depression, and stress have been screaming in silence. Heal his emotions where betrayal, rejection, and shame have left scars. Heal his finances where cycles of lack and fear have kept him bound. And most of all, heal his self-image the way he talks to himself, the way he sees himself when he looks in the mirror. Let him stop bleeding in places no one else even knows are wounded.

You said healing is the children's bread, so today let him eat and be filled. Let him taste full restoration not just patched up, not just coping, but completely renewed, inside and out. Let this be the day of a new beginning, not just healing for him, but healing that flows through him and blesses generations after him.

Thank You, God, that he will walk whole, restored, and free.
Amen.

Scripture Reading:

"For I will restore health to you, and your wounds I will heal, declares the Lord." — Jeremiah 30:17 (ESV)

Today's Challenge:

Write down one area of your life that still hurts. Pray: *"God, I give this wound to You. Make me whole again."* Then take one healing step today whether it is scheduling the appointment, reaching out for support, or giving yourself permission to rest.

Daily Reminder Quote:

"Healing is multi-dimensional, do not just settle for physical relief when your soul needs restoring too. You deserve to be whole." — Ebony N. Mayo

Journal Space:

(Write your healing prayer, reflect on what still hurts, or acknowledge how far you have already come.)

_____

_____

_____

_____

_____

_____

_____

_____

_____

_____

_____

_____

_____

COURAGE

(When Fear Tries to Win)

Reflection Question:

Where in your life do you need more courage? Is there a step you have been avoiding because of fear, uncertainty, or pain?

DEAR GOD, THANK YOU FOR THIS AMAZING MAN:

God, I thank You for this man's heart the way he shows up, even when he is afraid. Remind him today that courage does not mean he is never scared; it means he keeps moving despite the fear.

I pray for courage in every area of his life. Give him courage to speak truth, even when it is uncomfortable. Courage to walk away from what no longer serves him. Courage to pursue purpose over popularity, and courage to stand firm in the identity You have placed within him.

God, remind him that he is not weak or forgotten he is a man of valor. He is braver than the voices that try to shrink him, stronger than the lies that were spoken over him, and destined to rise above every label that was never his to carry. Speak into his spirit a new identity that overrides every word curse and every doubt he has ever believed.

Give him the courage to confront what he has been avoiding, to have the hard conversations, to face the mirror, to take the leap, to end the cycle, and to begin again. Whatever fear has been whispering in his ear, silence it with Your truth. Let him know his past does not disqualify him, his mistakes do not diminish him, and his story is still being written with redemption at the center.

If he has been stuck in shame, lift him out of it. If he has been paralyzed by fear of failure, breathe fresh wind into his sails. Let him know he is not what he has been through, he is who You are shaping him into. Remind him that courage is not always loud or dramatic; sometimes courage is choosing to stand, to stay, and to keep moving forward when everything in him wants to quit.

And in those quiet moments when he wonders if he has what it takes, whisper to his spirit: "You do. You are mine. I am with you. Now move."
Amen.

Scripture Reading:

"Have I not commanded you? Be strong and courageous. Do not be afraid; do not be discouraged, for the Lord your God will be with you wherever you go." — Joshua 1:9 (ESV)

Today's Challenge:

Write down one decision you have been afraid to make or one step you have been putting off. Pray: *"God, give me the courage to move even if I am scared."* Then take one small step toward it today.

Daily Reminder Quote:

"Courage is not the absence of fear, it is the refusal to let fear decide your future." — Ebony N. Mayo

Journal Space:

(Reflect on where courage is needed in your life. What are you being called to do that fear has delayed?)

_____

_____

_____

_____

_____

_____

_____

_____

_____

_____

_____

_____

_____

FINANCES

(Provision, Purpose & Peace)

Reflection Question:

How are your finances honestly? Are you managing what you have well? Are you positioned to receive and sustain the wealth you are praying for?

DEAR GOD, THANK YOU FOR THIS AMAZING MAN:

God, I lift up this man's financial life to You today. You see the pressure he feels to provide, to stretch every dollar, to build something meaningful with limited resources. You see when he is quiet about it, because pride would not let him ask for help. You see when the bank account is low, yet he still shows up with faith.

God, I pray You shift him from scarcity to abundance, and from abundance to overflow. Break the cycle of "just enough." Break the fear that says, "There is never going to be more." Break every generational mindset that normalizes lack, survival, and financial stress.

Heal his relationship with money. Remove the shame tied to past mistakes, overspending, under-earning, poor planning, or missed opportunities. If he is in a financial bind or struggling, remind him that his worth is not defined by his bank account. Help him to not feel less of a man because of his current circumstances.

Surround him with people who do not emasculate him or make him feel undervalued especially if he is earning less than what society says he is supposed to or still building his dream. Let him feel respected, seen, and supported, not judged.

Give him wisdom, strategy, and discipline to steward what he has now, while preparing him for the overflow that is ahead.

Let unexpected increase find him. Open doors for opportunities that multiply provision. Let his name be mentioned in places where favor is released. Send ideas, clients, promotions, raises, and opportunities that create streams of income not just for his comfort, but for his calling.

Make him the first in his family to build wealth without compromise. Not for vanity, but for legacy. Not for status, but for freedom. Not just for gain, but for impact.

Make him a lender, not a borrower. Make him a solution, not just a request. Make him a king who manages resources with humility, generosity, and grace.

And when wealth comes, God, do not let it change who he is. Let it only elevate what he can do, how he can give, and the lives he can transform.
Amen.

Scripture Reading:

"Bread is made for laughter, and wine gladdens life, and money answers everything." — Ecclesiastes 10:19 (ESV) "For the love of money is a root of all kinds of evils..." — 1 Timothy 6:10 (ESV)

Today's Challenge:

Look at your finances today without fear. Pray: *"God, give me wisdom to handle what I have and the strategy to grow what You are sending."* Commit to one small, wise financial step: budget, save, tithe, pay down debt, or seek wise counsel.

Daily Reminder Quote:

"There is nothing wrong with having money as long as the money does not have you." — Ebony N. Mayo

Journal Space:

(Reflect on your relationship with money past, present, and where you want it to go.)

_____

_____

_____

_____

_____

_____

_____

_____

_____

_____

_____

_____

_____

PATIENCE

(The Strength to Wait Without Breaking)

Reflection Question:

What are you currently waiting on? Is impatience causing you to force something that God is still forming?

DEAR GOD, THANK YOU FOR THIS AMAZING MAN:

God, I lift up this man today especially in the places where he has been waiting, praying, and hoping, yet still does not see the outcome. You know what he is believing for. You know how long he has been holding on. You know the number of times he has whispered, *"God, when is it going to happen for me?"*

I pray for patience, not the kind that folds its arms and gives up, but the kind that stands tall when life delays the dream. The kind that chooses peace while the process is still unfolding. The kind that trusts Your timing even when the clock says it is too late.

God, keep him from comparing his timeline to anyone else. Protect him from rushing what You are still refining. Remind him that slow does not mean stagnant, it means strategic. Show him that delay does not mean denial, it means preparation.

If he is weary from doing good, breathe strength back into him. If he is tempted to settle for less because waiting feels too heavy, stop him in his tracks. If he is close to giving up on what You told him to pursue, whisper Your promises again and rekindle his fire to believe.

Let patience do its work in him, maturing him, protecting him, and preparing him for the blessing that is on the way. Let him know he is not forgotten. You are not ignoring him. You are preparing something greater than what he would have settled for.

Thank You, God, for the unseen work happening right now in him, around him, and ahead of him.
Amen.

Scripture Reading:

"But let patience have her perfect work, that ye may be perfect and entire, wanting nothing." — James 1:4 (KJV)

Today's Challenge:

Think about one area of your life where you have been rushing. Pray: *"God, give me strength to wait without losing faith."* Then, practice patience today in a conversation, in a decision, or even in traffic.

Daily Reminder Quote:

"Sometimes the delay is not punishment, it is protection. Be patient. What is for you is still coming." — *Ebony N. Mayo*

Journal Space:

(Write about what you are waiting for and how waiting has tested or matured you. Be honest about the feelings and the lessons hidden in the waiting.)

_____

_____

_____

_____

_____

_____

_____

_____

_____

_____

_____

_____

_____

PROTECTION

(Covered, Watched Over & Guarded)

Reflection Question:

Where do you feel most vulnerable right now physically, emotionally, spiritually, or relationally? Have you been relying on your strength more than God's covering?

DEAR GOD, THANK YOU FOR THIS AMAZING MAN:

*G*od, today I ask You to surround this man with a hedge of protection. You see how much he carries. You see how often he shields others. He has stood guard for so many now, I pray You stand guard over him.

Cover his body keep him from sickness, injury, and fatigue. Cover his mind, silence anxiety, overthinking, and tormenting thoughts. Cover his heart protect him from betrayal, disappointment, and unseen attacks. Cover his family, his children, his relationships, his finances, his reputation, and his calling.

God, be his defender when opposition rises. Be his shield when life comes swinging. Be his refuge when the world is too loud and the load too heavy.

Even in the places he does not speak of the hidden vulnerabilities, the quiet fears cover him there, too. I plead the blood of Jesus over every detail of his life. Block every scheme meant to harm him. Confuse every enemy assignment. Cancel every hidden agenda designed to destroy his peace.

Guard his steps when he enters rooms and guard his feet from the rooms he should never enter. Keep him safe from traps he cannot see. Cover his back in conversations he is not part of.

And remind him: even though he is a protector, he is still worthy of being protected. Let him know it is not weakness to rest in Your covering, but wisdom.

When the weight feels unbearable, let him feel the safety of Your presence. He is divinely protected not by chance, not by luck, but by Your hand.

Let him rest tonight knowing You never sleep. Let him rise tomorrow with boldness, knowing angels go before him.

Thank You, God, for being his warrior, his watchman, and his wall of fire. Amen.

Scripture Reading:

"But the Lord is faithful, and He will strengthen you and protect you from the evil one." — 2 Thessalonians 3:3 (NIV) "No weapon formed against you shall prosper..." — Isaiah 54:17 (NKJV)

Today's Challenge:

Say this aloud before you leave your home today: *"I am protected. God has me covered."* Then pray over your home, your vehicle, your workplace, and your loved ones.

Daily Reminder Quote:

"You have been carrying the weight but God's been carrying you. You are covered." — *Ebony N. Mayo*

Journal Space:

(Reflect on the areas where you have felt exposed, unprotected, or under attack. Write about the times God's protection showed up even when you did not recognize it in the moment.)

_____

_____

_____

_____

_____

_____

_____

_____

_____

_____

_____

_____

_____

_____

DELIVERANCE

(Freedom from What has Been Holding You Back)

Reflection Question:

What habits, patterns, thoughts, or secret battles do you need God to deliver you from today?

DEAR GOD, THANK YOU FOR THIS AMAZING MAN:

*G*od, today I pray for deliverance in this man's life. You know the hidden battles he fights. The private struggles he does not talk about. The habits he has tried to break on his own. The thoughts that keep him bound. The cycles that keep repeating.

God, I pray You break every chain. Set him free from addictions, substances, porn, gambling, social media, unhealthy relationships, self-sabotage, or anything else that has become an idol in his life. Remind him that even the things society normalizes can become traps when they steal time, purpose, peace, and relationships.

Set him free from negative thinking and limiting beliefs that tell him he will never change or rise above his past. Set him free from generational curses patterns that ran through his family but end with him.

God, deliver him from anger that erupts without warning. Deliver him from unforgiveness that poisons his peace. Deliver him from fear that paralyzes his purpose. Deliver him from shame that keeps him silent.

Give him victory over every obstacle and stumbling block that may delay Your plan for his life.

You said in Your Word that who the Son sets free is free indeed. So today, let freedom rise up in his spirit. Let him walk in deliverance, not just as a moment, but as a lifestyle. Show him that freedom is possible. Remind him that he is not defined by his struggle, he is defined by Your redemption.

Give him the strength to surrender what he has been holding onto. Surround him with safe people and resources to walk out his deliverance in wisdom and accountability. God, do not just take the taste of bondage away, take the desire for it away. Fill those empty spaces with Your presence, Your purpose, and Your power.

Thank You, God, for being his Deliverer. For fighting battles he can not see. For loving him enough to free him and keep him free. Amen.

Scripture Reading:

"So if the Son sets you free, you will be free indeed." — John 8:36 (NIV)

Today's Challenge:

Write down one area where you need deliverance. Pray: *"God, I can not do this alone. Deliver me and give me the wisdom and support to walk in freedom."* Take one small step today toward accountability and lasting change.

Daily Reminder Quote:

"Your struggle is not your identity. God can deliver you and keep you free." — Ebony N. Mayo

Journal Space:

(Write honestly about what you are ready to let go of and what freedom would look like in your life.)

_____

_____

_____

_____

_____

_____

_____

_____

_____

_____

_____

_____

_____

_____

_____

GRACE

(Receiving What You Do Not Deserve & Giving What Others Do Not Earn)

Reflection Question:

Where in your life do you need to extend grace to yourself or others today? Have you been rejecting grace because you feel you do not deserve it?

DEAR GOD, THANK YOU FOR THIS AMAZING MAN:

God, today I thank You for the covering of grace over this man's life. Grace that woke him up this morning. Grace that kept him through dangers seen and unseen. Grace that forgave him for things he is still learning to forgive himself for.

God, remind him today that grace is not just what You give, grace is who You are. Help him to stop running from it. Help him to stop punishing himself for mistakes You already paid for. Release him from the guilt of what he did not know, what he could not control, and who he had to be in survival seasons.

God, let him also learn to extend grace outward to his children, to his partner, to his friends, and even to those who disappointed or hurt him. Remind him that extending grace does not excuse the wrong, it simply frees him from bitterness.

Let him see that grace does not make him weak, it makes him more like You. Shape his words today with grace. Shape his reactions today with grace. Shape his decisions today with grace. Make him a man who leaves people better than he found them not because they earned it, but because grace overflows from within him.

And when he feels unworthy, whisper to his spirit that Your grace is sufficient. That it covers his weakness, his failures, and his shortcomings. That it never runs out.

Thank You, God, for the grace that restores. For mercy that is new every morning. For love that refuses to let him stay the same. Amen.

Scripture Reading:

"But he said to me, 'My grace is sufficient for you, for my power is made perfect in weakness.'" — 2 Corinthians 12:9 (NIV)

Today's Challenge:

Think of one area where you have been hard on yourself or others. Pray: "God, help me to extend the same grace to myself and others that You extend to me." Practice it today and replace criticism with compassion.

Daily Reminder Quote:

"Grace is not about earning it, it is about receiving it, then giving it away." — *Ebony N. Mayo*

Journal Space:

(Write about where you need to receive grace and where you need to give it more freely.)

_____

_____

_____

_____

_____

_____

_____

_____

_____

_____

_____

_____

_____

_____

FOCUS

(Locking In On What Truly Matters)

Reflection Question:

What has been distracting you lately? Where do you need to refocus to align with your goals, your purpose, and your peace?

DEAR GOD, THANK YOU FOR THIS AMAZING MAN:

God, today I lift up this man's focus to You. You see how much pulls at him daily. Responsibilities, fears, opportunities, temptations, and the endless pressure to keep it all together. You see when his mind races at night, juggling unfinished tasks and unspoken worries. You see when he feels like no matter how much he gives, it is never enough.

God, calm his spirit right now. Quiet the distractions. Silence the noise. Bring his thoughts back into alignment with Your will.

Help him focus on what truly matters. Purpose over distraction, impact over busyness, and peace over chaos. Show him the difference between what is urgent and what is truly important. Teach him that "no" is a full sentence, and that every good opportunity is not always a God opportunity.

Where his vision has been foggy, give him clarity. Where he has been procrastinating, give him discipline. Where he has abandoned goals because of distraction, reignite his passion and consistency. If there are people or habits pulling him off course, give him wisdom, boundaries, and the strength to realign.

God, sharpen his focus like a warrior locking eyes on the target. Let him lock in so deeply that distractions lose their grip on him. Remind him that when his eyes stay fixed on You, everything else will fall into its rightful place.

Thank You for giving him a sound mind, a disciplined spirit, and a heart that beats for purpose.
Amen.

Scripture Reading:

"Set your minds on things above, not on earthly things." — Colossians 3:2 (NIV)

Today's Challenge:

Identify your top three priorities for today. Pray: "God, help me to focus on what matters and release what does not." Turn off one distraction, social media, TV, or unnecessary noise and use that time intentionally.

Daily Reminder Quote:

"Grace is not about earning it, it is about receiving it, then giving it away." — *Ebony N. Mayo*

Journal Space:

(Write about where your focus has been and where you need it to shift.)

_____

_____

_____

_____

_____

_____

_____

_____

_____

_____

_____

_____

_____

_____

FAVOR

(When God Opens Doors You Did not Knock On)

Reflection Question:

Where in your life do you need God's favor right now? Do you believe you are worthy of receiving favor or have you settled for struggle?

DEAR GOD, THANK YOU FOR THIS AMAZING MAN:

God, today I pray for favor over this man's life. You said in Your Word that favor surrounds him like a shield, and I declare that shield over every area of his journey.

Let Your favor go before him today into his workplace, into his business deals, into his interviews, negotiations, and projects. Let it follow him into his relationships, his finances, his family, and every room he walks into.

God, open doors he never even knocked on. Position his name in the hearts and minds of people who can bless him, partner with him, and help accelerate his purpose. Let favor speak for him when his resume can not. Let favor cover the places where his history would have counted him out and highlight the excellence You have placed within him.

I pray for *unusual favor, the* kind that turns "no" into "yes," that moves him from overlooked to chosen, that places him in rooms he never thought he would stand in. Favor that cannot be explained except by Your hand.

Remind him that favor is not about striving. It is about surrendering to Your sovereignty and trusting that You can accomplish in one moment what years of grinding could never achieve.

And remind him, God, that he is a King chosen, anointed, and worthy of divine favor. Favor does not make him who he is, it reveals who You created him to be.

Help him to walk humbly in favor not with arrogance, but with deep gratitude. And let him use that favor not just for himself, but to bless others, uplift his community, and expand Your kingdom.

Thank You, God, that Your favor lasts a lifetime, and no man, system, or circumstance can block what You have already ordained.
Amen.

Scripture Reading:

"For You, O Lord, will bless the righteous; with favor You will surround him as with a shield." — Psalm 5:12 (NKJV)

Today's Challenge:

Pray specifically for favor in one area of your life today. Say aloud: *"God's favor surrounds me like a shield. Doors are opening for me that no man can shut."* Then walk in confidence that His favor is already working on your behalf.

Daily Reminder Quote:

"One moment of God's favor can do more for you than years of grinding alone." — Ebony N. Mayo

Journal Space:

(Write about the areas where you need favor and reflect on moments when God's favor has already shown up in your life.)

_____

_____

_____

_____

_____

_____

_____

_____

_____

_____

_____

_____

_____

WISDOM

(The Blueprint for Every Decision)

Reflection Question:

Where in your life do you need God's wisdom right now? Are you making decisions out of emotion or divine direction?

DEAR GOD, THANK YOU FOR THIS AMAZING MAN:

*G*od, today I pray for wisdom over this man's life. You see every decision before him, the ones he speaks about and the ones he silently carries. You know the choices that will shape his future, his family, his finances, his health, his business, and his relationships.

God, give him wisdom beyond his years. Wisdom that silences confusion. Wisdom that shuts down distraction. Wisdom that shields him from traps he cannot see. Wisdom that aligns his steps with Your will and not just his wants.

Help him to pause before reacting. Help him to seek You before deciding. Help him to discern the difference between good ideas and God ideas.

Let him walk in wisdom that produces peace, not chaos. Strategy, not striving. Progress, not setbacks.

You promised in Your Word that if any man lacks wisdom and asks, You will give it generously. So today, God, I ask that You pour out wisdom on him like oil. Anoint his mind to think clearly. Anoint his ears to recognize Your voice above the noise. Anoint his eyes to see the path You have already prepared for him.

Let wisdom govern his leadership. Let wisdom shape his words. Let wisdom direct his finances, his investments, his relationships, his time, and his energy.

Make him a man who is remembered for wise decisions, decisions that build legacy, guard his peace, and honor Your kingdom. And when he does not know what to do, remind him that the wisest move he can ever make is to seek You first.

God, let him walk as a King who not only carries power but carries wisdom because wisdom will sustain the crown You have placed on his head. Thank You for being his Wonderful Counselor, his guide, and his ever-present source of truth.
Amen.

Scripture Reading:

"If any of you lacks wisdom, let him ask of God, who gives to all liberally and without reproach, and it will be given to him." — James 1:5 (NKJV)

Today's Challenge:

Think of one decision you are facing right now. Pray: *"God, give me Your wisdom and clarity today."* Pause, listen, and write down what comes to your spirit.

Daily Reminder Quote:

"Wisdom is not just knowing what to do, it is knowing when, how, and if you should do it at all." — Ebony N. Mayo

Journal Space:

(Write about the decisions you are currently facing and the wisdom you are asking God for today.)

_____

_____

_____

_____

_____

_____

_____

_____

_____

_____

_____

_____

_____

_____

TIME

(*Your Most Valuable Non-Renewable Resource*)

Reflection Question:

How are you spending your time? Are your daily habits building your future or just filling your days?

DEAR GOD, THANK YOU FOR THIS AMAZING MAN:

*G*od, today I pray over this man's time. You see the hours he pours into work, family, responsibilities, and dreams. You also see the moments that slip away unnoticed. Teach him to number his days and to understand that every minute matters.

Show him where distractions are stealing from his destiny. Show him where old habits are draining energy instead of fueling growth. Expose the places where busyness has disguised itself as progress but has left him feeling empty.

God, help him to use his time with wisdom and intention. Let him rest without guilt, and work with diligence. Let him build habits that give life, not burnout. Let him be fully present in the moments that matter most with his children, his partner, his loved ones so they feel his presence, not just his provision.

Redeem the time he feels he lost through mistakes, delays, or missed opportunities. Remind him that You are the God who restores years and multiplies what seems too little. Show him how to shift from wasting time to investing time in his faith, his health, his family, his vision, and his legacy.

And when life feels rushed, God, remind him to pause. To breathe. To anchor himself in You. Because time with You is never wasted, it is the foundation for everything else.

Thank You, God, for the gift of today. Help him to steward it well. Amen.

Scripture Reading:

"Teach us to number our days, that we may gain a heart of wisdom." — *Psalm 90:12 (NIV)*

Today's Challenge:

Audit your time today. Pray: *"God, help me use my time wisely and align my days with Your purpose."* Write down one thing you will stop doing and one thing you will start doing to better steward your time.

Daily Reminder Quote:

"Time is your most valuable investment. Spend it on what builds your future and feeds your soul." — *Ebony N. Mayo*

Journal Space:

(Reflect on how you have been spending your time and where you want to be more intentional.)

_____

_____

_____

_____

_____

_____

_____

_____

_____

_____

_____

_____

_____

GRATITUDE

(The Power of a Thankful Heart)

Reflection Question:

What are 10 things big or small you are grateful for right now? Do you let gratitude shape your perspective daily, even in hard seasons?

DEAR GOD, THANK YOU FOR THIS AMAZING MAN:

*G*od, today I pray that gratitude would rise up in this man's heart. Teach him to see blessings even in the midst of battles. Help him to notice the small wins, the answered prayers he forgot he once prayed for, the quiet mercies that meet him every morning.

God, I thank You for his breath, his health, his family, his provision, and the very fact that he woke up today with purpose. But more than the obvious, remind him to be grateful for the lessons in loss, the strength in struggle, the wisdom that only comes from experience.

When discouragement whispers that he does not have enough, remind him of everything he already carries. When comparison tells him he is behind, remind him of how far he has actually come. When his heart feels heavy with what is missing, let gratitude shift his focus to what is present.

God, let gratitude be his perspective, not just a passing thought. Let it guard his mind when worry creeps in. Let it soften his heart when anger tries to rise. Let it anchor his spirit when storms are raging.

Gratitude is a weapon and today, I pray he uses it. Instead of replaying disappointments, let him replay Your goodness. Instead of focusing on what is broken, let him celebrate what is still standing. Instead of waiting for everything to be perfect, let him give thanks right now, right here.

Thank You, God, for reminding him that gratitude does not deny pain it redefines it. That even when life feels heavy, there is always something to be thankful for.
Amen.

Scripture Reading:

"Give thanks in all circumstances; for this is God's will for you in Christ Jesus." — *1 Thessalonians 5:18 (NIV)*

Today's Challenge:

Make a gratitude list of 10 things you are thankful for today. Pray: *"God, thank You for what I have, for where I am, and for what You are still doing in my life."* Read it out loud and carry it with you into your day.

Daily Reminder Quote:

"Gratitude does not change your circumstances. It changes how you see them. And when your perspective shifts, so does your life." — Ebony N. Mayo

Journal Space:

(Write out your gratitude list. Reflect on how gratitude shifts your perspective, even in the middle of challenges.)

_____

_____

_____

_____

_____

_____

_____

_____

_____

_____

_____

_____

_____

_____

FAITHFULNESS

(Consistency When No One is Watching)

Where in your life do you need to be more faithful right now? In relationships, finances, health, prayer, commitments, or purpose?

DEAR GOD, THANK YOU FOR THIS AMAZING MAN:

God, today I pray for this man's faithfulness. You see his strengths and his struggles. You know the areas where he shows up consistently and the areas where he has been wavering, distracted, or discouraged.

God, teach him the power of faithfulness. Remind him that greatness is not built overnight, it is built daily, through small decisions done with excellence and integrity. Help him to stay committed even when it feels unnoticed. Help him to keep showing up even when no one applauds. Help him to stay the course even when progress feels slow.

God, I pray for faithfulness in his relationships. That he would honor his commitments and show up as a man of his word. Faithfulness in his finances, that he would steward what he has with wisdom, generosity, and discipline. Faithfulness in his health, that he would care for the body You have given him as a vessel for purpose. Faithfulness in his work, that he would work with diligence and excellence, serving as if working directly for You. Faithfulness in his spiritual life, that he would remain anchored in prayer, in Your Word, and in Your presence no matter how busy life gets.

God, let his faithfulness produce fruit in every area. Show him that consistency is a form of worship. Remind him that what he does today shapes who he becomes tomorrow. Strengthen his will when distractions call his name. Strengthen his discipline when excuses try to rise up. Strengthen his integrity when shortcuts seem tempting.

Thank You, God, for being faithful even when we are faithless. Help him to mirror that faithfulness to everyone and everything You have entrusted to him.
Amen.

Scripture Reading:

"A faithful man will abound with blessings..." — Proverbs 28:20 (NKJV)

Today's Challenge:

Identify one area where you have lacked consistency. Pray: *"God, help me to be faithful in this area today."* Take one action step, however small, that shows faithfulness.

Daily Reminder Quote:

"Faithfulness is not about feelings, it is about choosing to show up even when it's hard." — Ebony N. Mayo

Journal Space:

(Reflect on where you have been faithful and where you need to build consistency and integrity.)

_____

_____

_____

_____

_____

_____

_____

_____

_____

_____

_____

_____

_____

LEADERSHIP

(Leading with Integrity, Strength, and Humility)

Reflection Question:

Where are you called to lead right now? Are you leading from a place of service, character, and vision or just position and control?

DEAR GOD, THANK YOU FOR THIS AMAZING MAN:

*G*od, I lift up the leader inside of this man today. Whether he realizes it or not, someone is watching him, learning from him, and following his example. It might be his children, his family, his team, his friends, or his community but You placed leadership in his DNA.

God, help him lead with integrity. Let his choices reflect honor. Let his words build, not break. Let his presence inspire confidence and character in others.

Help him lead with humility. Teach him to listen before he speaks, to seek understanding before he reacts, and to remember that real leadership is not about power, it is about service. Remind him that titles fade, but character lasts forever.

God, give him strength to lead well. Strength to stand firm when pressure rises. Strength to make hard decisions with wisdom. Strength to stay steady when others would quit.

Remind him that leadership is not control, it is stewardship. People are not possessions, they are assignments. His role is not to dominate, but to equip, to protect, and to guide.

God, give him vision. Vision that looks beyond the moment and builds for the future. Vision that inspires others to rise, to dream, and to push past their own limits. Surround him with wise counsel and accountability so he always has sharpeners in his corner.

Protect his leadership from pride, insecurity, manipulation, and burnout. Keep his motives pure, his heart clean, and his spirit grounded in You.

Thank You, God, for trusting him with influence. Let him leave a legacy that speaks louder than his position, one that proves he was a man who led with honor, humility, and love.
Amen.

Scripture Reading:

"But among you it will be different. Whoever wants to be a leader among you must be your servant." — Matthew 20:26 (NLT)

Today's Challenge:

Identify one way you can serve someone you lead today. Pray: "God, teach me to lead with humility, integrity, and courage." Take that action before the day ends.

Daily Reminder Quote:

"Leadership is not about being in charge, it is about taking care of those in your charge." — Ebony N. Mayo

Journal Space:

(Write about your leadership strengths, your growth areas, and who you are called to lead in this season.)

_____

_____

_____

_____

_____

_____

_____

_____

_____

_____

_____

_____

_____

_____

INTEGRITY

(Who You Are When No One is Watching)

Reflection Question:

Are there areas in your life where your words and actions do not align? Where is God calling you to higher integrity today?

DEAR GOD, THANK YOU FOR THIS AMAZING MAN:

God, today I pray for integrity in this man's life. Help him to be the same man in private that he is in public. Help him to stand firm in his values even when compromise seems easier. Help him to live in such a way that his children, his family, his team, and his community see him as a man of unshakable character.

God, convict him gently when his words and actions do not align. Expose anything hidden that could destroy his reputation, his relationships, or his purpose. Not to shame him, but to free him from anything that would hold him back.

Give him the courage to choose honesty over deceit. To keep his promises even when it is hard. To do the right thing even when no one will ever know. To honor his commitments to his partner, his family, his finances, and his spiritual walk with the integrity of a true man of God.

Remind him that integrity is not just about what he avoids, but about what he builds. That his name carries weight. That his character opens doors which charisma never could. That integrity will keep him standing long after talent, money, or status fade away.

Let him be a man others can trust. Let his yes be yes and his no be no. Let his life reflect Your truth so clearly that others see Your glory through his choices.

Thank You, God, for shaping him into a man of strength, honor, and unwavering integrity.
Amen.

Scripture Reading:

"Whoever walks in integrity walks securely, but whoever takes crooked paths will be found out." — Proverbs 10:9 (NIV)

Today's Challenge:

Think about one area in your life where you have been tempted to cut corners. Pray: "God, give me strength to walk in integrity even when it costs me comfort." Commit to honoring your values in that area today.

Daily Reminder Quote:

"Integrity is doing the right thing even when it is hard and even when no one sees but God." — Ebony N. Mayo

Journal Space:

(Write about what integrity means to you and where God is calling you to higher standards right now.)

_____

_____

_____

_____

_____

_____

_____

_____

_____

_____

_____

_____

_____

OBEDIENCE

(Saying Yes Even When It is Hard)

Reflection Question:

Where is God calling you to obey right now? Are you delaying obedience out of fear, comfort, or pride?

DEAR GOD, THANK YOU FOR THIS AMAZING MAN:

*G*od, today I pray for this man's obedience. Not the kind that comes when it is easy or convenient but the kind that requires him to lay down pride, break old patterns, and step into the unknown.

Help him to hear Your voice clearly and respond without hesitation. Break the cycle of delayed obedience, and remind him that delayed obedience is still disobedience.

God, give him courage to obey even when the road feels unclear. Even when You ask him to leave what feels familiar. Even when You call him to forgive where there is deep hurt, to give when it feels like he has little left, to love where bitterness has tried to live, or to stand firm even if it means standing alone.

Show him that Your instructions are not restrictions, they are protections. That obedience is not about losing freedom, it is about walking fully in it. That every yes shapes him into the man You are calling him to be.

Remove rebellion and resistance from his heart. Replace it with humility, trust, and surrender. And when fear tries to make him stall, whisper to his spirit: "You can trust Me with this."

God, if there are places in his life where he has been wrestling with You, meet him there today. Remind him that You do not ask for his obedience to break him down, You ask for it to build him up. To position him for blessings, protection, favor, and growth.

Thank You for being patient with him when he has struggled to say yes. Thank You for never giving up on him as he learns to walk in full alignment with You. And thank You for the blessings already waiting on the other side of his obedience.
Amen.

Scripture Reading:

"If you are willing and obedient, you shall eat the good of the land."
— Isaiah 1:19 (NKJV)

Today's Challenge:

Identify one area where you have been resisting God's instruction. Pray: "God, give me the courage to obey You fully today." Then take at least one step of obedience before the end of the day.

Daily Reminder Quote:

"Obedience is not about understanding every detail, it is about trusting the One who does." — Ebony N. Mayo

Journal Space:

(Write about what obedience looks like in your life right now and where you are being called higher.)

_____

_____

_____

_____

_____

_____

_____

_____

_____

_____

_____

_____

_____

FORGIVENESS

(Letting Go to Live Free)

Reflection Question:

Who do you need to forgive today, including yourself? What pain are you still holding onto that God is asking you to release?

DEAR GOD, THANK YOU FOR THIS AMAZING MAN:

*G*od, today I pray about forgiveness in this man's life. You know the hurt he carries, the betrayals that cut deep, the words that wounded, the disappointments that still echo in his mind. You know how heavy it feels to hold on to pain when what he really longs for is peace.

God, I pray You give him the grace to forgive. To release the bitterness. To release the resentment. To release the mental and emotional chains that have tried to keep him bound to the past.

I pray he forgives himself too. For mistakes made in ignorance or anger. For decisions he regrets. For seasons where he did not show up as his best self. Help him to see that forgiveness does not erase accountability, but it does release shame.

God, I also pray for the hard kind of forgiveness, forgiving those who are no longer here, but who left wounds that still linger. Help him to release what was never resolved, what was left unsaid, and what can never be undone. Heal those hidden places, God, so he does not keep reliving pain that has already passed.

Soften his heart where it has grown cold and guarded. Remind him that forgiveness is not weakness, it is strength. That it takes a true man of valor to let go and move forward in peace.

And God, if forgiveness feels impossible right now, meet him in that place. Whisper to him that unforgiveness only poisons his own soul. Give him Your perspective, and fill every place emptied by unforgiveness with Your healing and love. Restore what was broken and redeem what was lost.

Thank You, God, for forgiving him fully and freely. Help him to extend that same forgiveness today to others and to himself.
Amen.

Scripture Reading:

"Be kind to one another, tenderhearted, forgiving one another, as God in Christ forgave you." — Ephesians 4:32 (ESV)

Today's Challenge:

Write down one name or your own that you need to forgive today. Pray: "God, help me release this pain and walk in forgiveness and freedom." Speak out loud: "I choose to forgive."

Daily Reminder Quote:

"Forgiveness is not saying what they did was okay, it is saying you are done letting it control your life." — Ebony N. Mayo

Journal Space:

(Write about who you are forgiving, past or present, why it has been hard, and what freedom would feel like.)

_____

_____

_____

_____

_____

_____

_____

_____

_____

_____

_____

_____

_____

FEAR

(Breaking Free from What Tries to Control You)

Reflection Question:

What fears have been keeping you up at night or holding you back from fully living? Which ones do you need God to silence today?

DEAR GOD, THANK YOU FOR THIS AMAZING MAN:

God, today I lift up every fear that has tried to take root in this man's heart. The fear of loss. The fear of failing. The fear of not being the best he can be. The fear of not being enough. God, You see the silent battles, the doubts about his future, his self-esteem, his purpose, his money, his family, his health, his relationships, his happiness.

I come against every lie of fear that whispers, "You can not," "You will not," "You are not." Replace those lies with Your truth. Remind him that You have not given him a spirit of fear, but of power, love, and a sound mind.

God, calm his fear of failure and remind him that failure is not final, its formation. Calm his fear of not having enough and show him that provision is already written into his destiny. Calm his fear of not being happy and remind him that joy is not in things, but in You. Calm his fear of relationships of being hurt, of not being loved, of not being chosen and surround him with love that is safe, genuine, and lasting.

God, speak to the fear he carries as a father, a husband, a leader. Fear of letting his children down. Fear of not leading his family well. Fear of repeating cycles. Remind him that with You, he is fully equipped for the role he has been given.

Speak to his fear about career and calling. When he wonders if he is in the right place, doing the right thing, or if he is wasting time, remind him that his steps are ordered and You waste nothing.

Speak to his fear about health and comparison. Remind him that his body is a temple, his journey is unique, and he does not have to measure his life against anyone else. Comparison is a thief, God, silence it.

Today, I declare fear broken off his life. Fear will not paralyze his purpose. Fear will not rob his joy. Fear will not keep him from love, success, healing, or peace. God, let courage rise in him like never before. Let confidence be his shield and faith be his weapon. Let him walk boldly into every area of his life, knowing You have already gone before him.

Thank You, God, that fear has no power where Your perfect love abides. Thank You that this man is not bound by fear he is free, he is chosen, he is equipped, and he is enough.
Amen.

Scripture Reading:

"For God has not given us a spirit of fear, but of power and of love and of a sound mind." — 2 Timothy 1:7 (NKJV)

Today's Challenge:

Identify one fear that has been holding you back. Pray: "God, I release this fear to You and choose courage instead." Take one small step today that fear has been trying to stop you from taking.

Daily Reminder Quote:

"Fear is loud, but faith is louder. You are not bound by fear, you are built for courage." — *Ebony N. Mayo*

Journal Space:

(Write about the fears you have been carrying and what life could look like without them.)

_____

_____

_____

_____

_____

_____

_____

_____

_____

_____

_____

_____

_____

_____

_____

WEALTH

(Building Legacy Beyond a Paycheck)

Reflection Question:

How do you view wealth? Is money your master or your tool? Are you building for now or for generations to come?

DEAR GOD, THANK YOU FOR THIS AMAZING MAN:

*G*od, today I pray over this man's wealth. Thank You for every resource You have already provided. Thank You for the mind You have given him to create, earn, build, and steward well.

God, I pray You break every poverty mindset in his life. Every lie that tells him there will never be enough. Every fear that makes him hoard instead of sow. Every generational curse that normalized lack, struggle, and financial chaos.

Replace it with an abundant mindset. One that believes there is always more in You. One that sees opportunities instead of obstacles. One that understands wealth is not just for comfort, but for calling. One that builds legacy, not just lifestyle. One that blesses others and funds kingdom work on earth.

God, give him strategy for wealth-building. Ideas, inventions, investments, promotions, and opportunities that position him to prosper. Give him discipline to manage what he earns. Give him generosity to give freely. Give him wisdom to multiply what You have placed in his hands.

Help him not to chase money, but to attract provision by pursuing purpose. Help him to see money as a tool, not an idol. Help him to walk in financial integrity, paying debts, honoring commitments, and making decisions that build stability and peace for his family.

God, I pray he becomes the first in his family to break cycles of financial struggle. Let his children's children benefit from the choices he makes today. Let him teach them principles of wealth, stewardship, generosity, faith, and abundance.

Thank You, God, for being his ultimate Source. Everything he has comes from You and with You, there is always more than enough. Amen.

Scripture Reading:

"But remember the Lord your God, for it is he who gives you the ability to produce wealth." — Deuteronomy 8:18 (NIV)

Today's Challenge:

Evaluate your current financial habits. Pray: "God, give me wisdom to build wealth that honors You and blesses others." Take one step today toward better stewardship, budgeting, saving, investing, giving, or planning.

Daily Reminder Quote:

"Wealth is not just about what you have, it is about what you build, who you bless, and the legacy you leave. Abundance is your birthright, walk in it." — Ebony N. Mayo

Journal Space:

(Write about your vision for wealth, what financial freedom would look like, and how you want to use it for God's glory.)

_____

_____

_____

_____

_____

_____

_____

_____

_____

_____

_____

_____

_____

_____

HUMILITY

(Staying Grounded No Matter How High You Rise)

Reflection Question:

Where is pride showing up in your life? Where do you need to humble yourself before God and others today?

DEAR GOD, THANK YOU FOR THIS AMAZING MAN:

God, today I pray for humility in this man's life. You see his strengths, his achievements, and his progress. You see the confidence he carries but You also see the pride that sometimes tries to attach itself to that confidence.

God, keep him humble. Help him to remember that everything he has comes from You, his gifts, his opportunities, his platform, his influence. Remind him that without Your breath in his lungs, he is nothing.

God, I ask that You protect him from the distractions that try to pull him away from humility. Do not let money consume him. Do not let women, devices, pride, or arrogance take him off course. Guard his heart so he does not mistake blessings for entitlement or confuse influence with control.

Teach him that humility is not weakness, it is wisdom. It is strength under control. It is knowing that he does not need to boast about himself when You are the One who exalts in due season.

Help him to serve without seeking applause. To give without expecting recognition. To listen without needing to be right. To apologize without defending his pride.

God, strip away any arrogance that tries to take root in his heart. Expose prideful thoughts that would keep him from growth, connection, and intimacy with You. Replace them with a humble spirit, one that remains teachable, gracious, and steady no matter how much success he reaches.

Let humility open doors that pride would have slammed shut. Let it attract wise counsel, strong relationships, and favor that lasts. And remind him daily that Jesus the King of Kings stooped low to wash feet. Help him to carry that same posture of servant leadership every day.

Thank You for the example of humility in Christ. Shape him into a man who honors You through humble strength, grounded character, and a heart that seeks to glorify You above himself.
Amen.

Scripture Reading:

"Humble yourselves, therefore, under God's mighty hand, that he may lift you up in due time." — 1 Peter 5:6 (NIV)

Today's Challenge:

Identify an area where pride has shown up in your life. Pray: "God, help me to humble myself and walk in wisdom today." Take one action today that reflects humility, listening, apologizing, serving, or honoring someone else.

Daily Reminder Quote:

"Humility does not lower your worth, it elevates your wisdom and deepens your impact." — Ebony N. Mayo

Journal Space:

(Write about where you are being called to deeper humility and what that looks like practically.)

_____

_____

_____

_____

_____

_____

_____

_____

_____

_____

_____

_____

_____

_____

_____

VULNERABILITY

(The Courage to Be Seen and Known)

Reflection Question:

Do you allow yourself to be vulnerable, to be honest about your struggles, fears, or emotions? Or have you been hiding behind strength because you fear judgment or rejection?

DEAR GOD, THANK YOU FOR THIS AMAZING MAN:

*G*od, today I pray over this man's heart the places he has hidden because the world told him he had to always be strong. For the tears he has held back. For the fears he has buried. For the questions he has been too afraid to ask. God, remind him that vulnerability is not weakness it is strength. That true courage is not pretending he has it all together, but admitting when he does not.

Heal the parts of him that were taught to shut down his emotions. Break the lies that told him real men do not cry, do not ask for help, do not show pain. Remind him that even Jesus wept, even Jesus asked for support, even Jesus showed His wounds.

God, give him safe spaces where he can lay down the weight. Friends who would not mock him. A partner who will not weaponize his honesty. A brotherhood that holds him up when he feels weak. And above all, remind him that he can always be vulnerable with You because You already know every hidden thought and secret battle.

God, I pray he finds freedom in honesty. That he learns it is okay to say, "I need help." It is okay to admit, "I am not okay." It is okay to confess, "I can not do this alone." Let him see that vulnerability does not take away his masculinity, it deepens it. It makes him a better father, a stronger leader, a more loving partner, and a more faithful son of God.

Thank You, God, that when he chooses to be vulnerable, You cover him, not expose him. You strengthen him, not shame him. You heal him, not harm him.
Amen.

Scripture Reading:

"My grace is sufficient for you, for my power is made perfect in weakness." — 2 Corinthians 12:9 (NIV)

Today's Challenge:

Be vulnerable in one area today. Share honestly with God, a trusted friend, or write openly in your journal. Speak one truth you have been afraid to say out loud.

Daily Reminder Quote:

"Vulnerability is not weakness, it is the doorway to healing, connection, and real strength." — Ebony N. Mayo

Journal Space:

(Write honestly about where you have struggled to be vulnerable and how God may be calling you to open up.)

_____

_____

_____

_____

_____

_____

_____

_____

_____

_____

_____

_____

_____

EXPERIENCED ABUSE

(Healing From Hurt, Rising in Strength)

Reflection Question:

What type of abuse have you experienced in your life? Did it make you an abuser? Do you feel you are a victim or victor?

DEAR GOD, THANK YOU FOR THIS AMAZING MAN:

*G*od, I lift up every wound caused by people who were supposed to love and protect him. I pray over the abuse he experienced whether verbal, spiritual, physical, emotional, or sexual. Touch the little boy inside of him who was silenced, ignored, or dismissed when he tried to cry out for help. Heal the places where his innocence was stolen, where he was molested, touched in ways no child should ever be touched, or disrespected sexually in ways that planted shame and confusion. Restore the parts of him that still carry the weight of words that cut too deep, hands that hurt instead of held, and love that was twisted into something painful.

God, I bind the spirits of rejection, abandonment, and broken trust that came as a result of his abuse. I rebuke the cycle of pain that tries to repeat itself in his life. What happened to him was wrong. It may have been hidden, silenced, or minimized but You see it all, and You are greater than it all.

Reverse the lies, perversion, and false beliefs planted in him by that trauma. Wash him clean. Renew his mind, body, and spirit as if the abuse never happened. Break the chains that have tried to follow him into adulthood: fear, anger, shame, and secrecy. Make him whole, free, and unchained.

If he ever crosses paths with his abuser again, cover him with divine protection, strength, and healing. Give him the courage to walk in forgiveness not to excuse what was done, but to release himself from its grip. Guard his heart so that the pain of yesterday never dictates the promise of his tomorrow.

Remind him that he is not a victim. He is a victor. He is a survivor. He is an overcomer. His story is not one of shame, but of resilience, strength, and redemption. And God, whisper to his soul: "I am so proud of you, King."
Amen.

Scripture Reading:

"The Lord is a refuge for the oppressed, a stronghold in times of trouble." — Psalm 9:9–10 (NIV) "I will say of the Lord, 'He is my refuge and my fortress, my God, in whom I trust.'" — Psalm 91:2 (NIV)

Today's Challenge:

Write a letter to your younger self, the little boy who was hurt, reminding him that he is safe now, loved, and worthy of healing. Be honest about the pain you experienced and speak life over yourself as the man you are becoming. Declare out loud: "I am not what happened to me. I am a survivor, I am an overcomer, and I walk in victory."

Daily Reminder Quote:

"Children with dreams who experience unresolved childhood trauma grow up to be adults with nightmares."— Ebony N. Mayo

Journal Space:

(Reflect on the abuse you experienced. How has it shaped you? Where do you still need healing? How do you see yourself moving from victim to victor?)

_____

_____

_____

_____

_____

_____

_____

_____

_____

_____

_____

_____

_____

DEPRESSION

(*Light Breaking Through the Darkness*)

Reflection Question:

Have you not been feeling like yourself lately? Have you ever felt depressed or suicidal?

DEAR GOD, THANK YOU FOR THIS AMAZING MAN:

God, today I lift up this man who has carried silent battles that few may ever know. Society told him that "men do not cry," "men must always be strong," "men do not show emotion," and "men do not go to therapy." But today I cancel every lie and every word curse that has tried to silence his pain and keep him bound.

God, I come against every spirit of depression, heaviness, darkness, and loneliness. I release Your freedom, joy, peace, and hope into his life. Where numbness has tried to steal his fire, breathe fresh passion again. Where heaviness has weighed him down, lift him with Your strength. Where despair has whispered that life is not worth living, silence it with Your truth.

God, I pray for the nights when he just wants to sleep his pain away. For the mornings when he questioned if waking up even mattered. For the moments when suicidal thoughts crept in. For the seasons when unhealthy coping mechanisms felt easier than facing the pain. Remind him that even in those places, You were with him. He was never alone.

God, when his mood sinks without explanation and when isolation feels safer than connection, wrap him in Your arms. Send safe people who will see past the smile and reach for his heart. Show him the triggers, the habits, or the relationships that feed the weight of depression and give him courage to seek the help, resources, and healing he needs.

Remind him he is not powerless. Depression is not his identity. Hopelessness is not his future. He does not have to drift through life numb, heavy, or broken. Breathe new life into him, God. Lift him out of the pit and remind him that his story is not over. Replace despair with hope. Replace darkness with light. Replace shame with grace.

God, let him know there is no weakness in needing help. Therapy, counseling, prayer, and brotherhood these are lifelines, not empty labels. Protect his mind from the lies of the enemy and flood his spirit with Your peace that surpasses understanding.

Thank You, God, that even in the valley of depression, Your light breaks through. And today, I declare: his life matters, his purpose matters, and his tomorrow will be brighter than his yesterday.
Amen.

Scripture Reading:

"The righteous cry out, and the Lord hears them; He delivers them from all their troubles. The Lord is close to the brokenhearted and saves those who are crushed in spirit." — Psalm 34:17–18 (NIV)

Today's Challenge:

Be honest about your emotions today, even if only to yourself. Pray: "God, shine light into the dark places of my heart." Reach out: Call a trusted friend, mentor, or brother and be honest about how you are feeling. Seek support: If needed, schedule an appointment with a therapist. Taking that step is not weakness, it's wisdom. Move your body: Go for a walk, hit the gym, or stretch. Physical movement helps fight the weight of depression. Protect your mind: Limit time watching the news and social media, instead replace it with prayer, journaling, or listening to life-giving messages.

Daily Reminder Quote:

"Depression is a heavy weight, but God is a heavy weight lifter. And whether you know it yet or not, YOU are a heavy weight champ." — Ebony N. Mayo

Journal Space:

(Write about how depression has shown up in your life and what steps you can take to bring light back into your days.)

_____

_____

_____

_____

_____

_____

_____

_____

_____

_____

_____

_____

_____

_____

HEALTH

(Your Body is a Temple, Not a Burden)

Reflection Question:

How are you taking care of your body right now? What habits need to change for you to live a longer, stronger, healthier life?

DEAR GOD, THANK YOU FOR THIS AMAZING MAN:

God, today I pray over this man's health. Thank You for the body You have given him, strong, capable, and designed for purpose. Forgive him for the times he has neglected it, whether from busyness, stress, or unhealthy choices. Remind him that his body is not a burden, but a temple worthy of care, discipline, and respect.

God, strengthen his immune system and protect him from sickness, disease, and hidden ailments. Heal the pain, inflammation, or chronic struggles he may be battling in silence. Give him wisdom to care for himself to rest, to fuel his body with what it needs, to move with consistency, and to make choices that extend his life instead of shorten it.

God, break every habit that harms him, addictions, overeating, neglect, or anything that steals from his vitality. Replace them with discipline, self-control, and the desire to honor his body as the vessel carrying his purpose.

Cover his mind too, Lord. Give him peace when anxiety rises, clarity when confusion sets in, and strength when depression or anger tries to overwhelm him. If he needs help, remind him there is no shame in seeking therapy, counseling, or brotherhood to lift him up.

And let his spiritual health remain strong, rooted in Your Word, anchored in prayer, and sustained by faith. Help him see that true health is not just about muscles or stamina, but about balance: body, mind, spirit, and soul working together in strength.

Thank You, God, for creating him whole. Let him walk in health that sustains his calling, live long enough to see legacy unfold, and stand strong enough to carry out everything You have placed inside him.
Amen.

Scripture Reading:

"Do you not know that your bodies are temples of the Holy Spirit, who is in you, whom you have received from God? You are not your own." — 1 Corinthians 6:19 (NIV)

Today's Challenge:

Identify one health habit you need to start or stop today. Pray: "God, give me discipline to care for my body as Your temple." Take one intentional step toward better health, such as exercise, water intake, quality sleep, or better nutrition.

Daily Reminder Quote:

"Your body is the only place you have to live, treat it like the temple it is." — Ebony N. Mayo

Journal Space:

(Write about your current health habits and what changes you want to make for a stronger future.)

_____

_____

_____

_____

_____

_____

_____

_____

_____

_____

_____

_____

_____

PEACE

(Calm in the Middle of Chaos)

Reflection Question:

Do you have true peace right now? Where is anxiety, fear, or anger stealing your calm and robbing your focus?

DEAR GOD, THANK YOU FOR THIS AMAZING MAN:

*G*od, today I pray for peace over this man's life. You see the storms he has been navigating, the battles in his mind, the pressures on his shoulders, the worries that keep him up at night. You see the chaos that tries to surround him, distract him, and break him down.

God, I speak Your supernatural peace over him right now. Peace that surpasses all understanding. Peace that anchors him when life feels unsteady. Peace that guards his heart and mind against fear, anxiety, and doubt.

God, calm his thoughts today. Silence the lies of the enemy that say he will not make it, that he is not enough, that things will never change. Remind him that You are his refuge and fortress. That even if everything around him falls apart, You remain unshaken.

Teach him that he does not have to strive for perfection. That he can rest in *Shalom*, Your perfect peace. Peace that covers his mistakes, his imperfections, and the parts of himself he still wrestles with. Peace that allows him to breathe, to be, and to trust You fully.

God, let Your peace reign in his home. In his relationships. In his finances. In his career decisions. In his body, his mind, and his spirit.

Help him to carry peace into every room he walks into. To respond instead of react. To choose stillness over striving. To rest in the truth that You are fighting battles he can not see.

Thank You, God, for being Jehovah Shalom, the Lord his Peace. Let him sleep deeply tonight knowing You are covering every detail of his life.
Amen.

Scripture Reading:

"Peace I leave with you; my peace I give you. I do not give to you as the world gives. Do not let your hearts be troubled and do not be afraid." — John 14:27 (NIV)

Today's Challenge:

Identify one area of your life that has been filled with anxiety or chaos. Pray: "God, I surrender this to You. Fill me with Your peace today." Take one action to protect your peace, such as prayer, silence, walking away from unnecessary conflict, or resting your mind.

Daily Reminder Quote:

"Peace is not found in perfect circumstances, it is found in trusting the God who controls them." — *Ebony N. Mayo*

Journal Space:

(Write about where you need peace today and what it would feel like to truly rest in God's promises.)

_____

_____

_____

_____

_____

_____

_____

_____

_____

_____

_____

_____

_____

CONFIDENCE

(*Walking Boldly in Who God Created You to Be*)

Reflection Question:

Where in your life are you lacking confidence? Are you basing your worth on what others say, or on what God says about you?

DEAR GOD, THANK YOU FOR THIS AMAZING MAN:

God, today I pray for this man's confidence. You see the places where he second-guesses himself. In his decisions, his leadership, his career, his finances, his looks, his body, his words, and even his worth.

You know the wounds that started long ago, the hurtful words spoken over him as a child. The teachers who told him he would not amount to anything. The family members who criticized more than encouraged. The former girlfriends, partners, spouses who broke him down instead of building him up. The opinions of others that still echo in his mind, making him feel like he is never enough.

God, today silence every lie that has been spoken over his life. Cancel every word curse that told him he was "too much" or "not enough." Remind him that his confidence does not come from their voices, it comes from Yours. He is not defined by rejection, ridicule, or regret. He is defined by being Your son, chosen, loved, redeemed, equipped, and intentionally designed.

When money is low, let him know his value has not changed. When he looks in the mirror and sees flaws, let him remember he was fearfully and wonderfully made. When he feels overlooked in relationships or doubted in his career, remind him that his worth is not up for debate.

Remove fear of failure from his mind. Remove comparison from his thoughts. Remove self-doubt from his heart. Replace them with courage, clarity, and unshakable confidence anchored in Your truth.

God, help him to walk boldly into rooms You have already called him to. To speak without shrinking. To carry himself with dignity whether he has much or little, whether he feels his best physically or is still working on his health. To stand tall in his convictions, even when others disagree. To show up fully as the man You created him to be without apology and without arrogance, but with authority.

Thank You, God, that his worth is not defined by his wallet, his weight, his wins, or the wounds of his past. It is defined by the fact that You breathed life into him and called him good. Let him carry himself today with quiet strength, bold faith, and unwavering confidence rooted in who he is in You.
Amen.

Scripture Reading:

"So do not throw away your confidence; it will be richly rewarded."
— Hebrews 10:35 (NIV)

Today's Challenge:

Write down one area where you have lacked confidence. Pray: "God, help me to see myself the way You see me and walk boldly in that truth today." Take one action that reflects confidence in that area before the day ends.

Daily Reminder Quote:

"Confidence is not thinking you are better than others, it is knowing you do not have to compare yourself to anyone." — Ebony N. Mayo

Journal Space:

Write about where you need more confidence: finances, health, relationships, career, or self-worth and what God says about you that silences insecurity. Also, write down words from your past that hurt you, then declare them broken over your life.

_____

_____

_____

_____

_____

_____

_____

_____

_____

_____

_____

_____

REDEMPTION

(Nothing is Beyond God's Power to Restore)

Reflection Question:

What area of your life feels too broken, lost, or wasted to redeem? Do you believe God can restore it beyond what you imagined?

DEAR GOD, THANK YOU FOR THIS AMAZING MAN:

God, today I pray for redemption in this man's life. Thank You that You are a God who redeems time, mistakes, losses, brokenness, and seasons that felt wasted.

God, You see the places in his life that feel beyond repair. The divorce that left him questioning if he could ever love or be loved again. The setbacks that made him feel like life passed him by. The job loss or failed business that shook his confidence and sense of security. The prison sentence that made him wonder if people would only see his past and not his potential. The nights of homelessness where he felt forgotten and unseen. The deep grief from losing a family member and the hole it left in his heart.

But today, God, I pray You breathe redemption into every area that feels dead. Remind him that nothing is too far gone for You. That You can restore what was stolen. That You can heal what was broken. That You can resurrect what was left for dead.

Redeem his time, the years he feels he wasted in fear, rebellion, or complacency. Redeem his finances, every bad decision, loss, or season of lack. Redeem his relationships, family connections, friendships, or love that was broken by pride, pain, or misunderstanding. Redeem his purpose, revive every dream You planted that he thought was over.

God, help him to forgive himself for the chapters he wishes he could rewrite. Help him release regret and walk forward in grace. Show him that his story is not finished, You are still writing it. And You promised that the latter will be greater than the former.

Thank You, God, that redemption is not about his perfection, but Your promise. Help him believe that You make all things new, including him. Let redemption rise in his life as proof that nothing is wasted in Your hands. It is repurposed.
Amen.

Scripture Reading:

"I will restore to you the years that the swarming locust has eaten…"
— Joel 2:25 (ESV)

Today's Challenge:

Write down one area of your life where you need God's redemption. Pray: "God, I give this to You. Redeem it in ways only You can." Take one small step today that aligns with believing God for restoration.

Daily Reminder Quote:

"Redemption means God takes what was meant to break you and uses it to build you stronger." — *Ebony N. Mayo*

Journal Space:

(Write about what you want God to redeem and what redemption would look like in your life.)

_____

_____

_____

_____

_____

_____

_____

_____

_____

_____

_____

_____

_____

DIRECTION

(Knowing Where to Go Next)

Reflection Question:

Where do you feel stuck, lost, or unsure right now? Have you truly asked God for direction and waited for His answer?

DEAR GOD, THANK YOU FOR THIS AMAZING MAN:

God, today I pray for direction in this man's life. You see where he is standing at crossroads, unsure which path to take. You see his desire to make the right decisions for his family, his future, his career, his finances, his relationships, and his purpose.

God, Your Word says that if he trusts You with all his heart and leans not on his own understanding, You will make his paths straight. So today, help him to surrender every plan, every fear, and every outcome to You.

Silence the confusion that clouds his thoughts. Remove the fear that makes him second-guess himself. God, speak clearly to his spirit today. Show him the next step even if You do not show him the whole journey.

Give him peace about where You are leading him, even when it does not look like what he expected. Give him faith to follow You fully, even when it requires leaving comfort behind.

God, I pray You block doors that are not meant for him. Redirect him if he is headed the wrong way. Close opportunities that would pull him off course, and open doors that align with Your will and his true purpose.

And God, help him to remember that Your timing is just as important as Your direction. If the answer has not come yet, it is not because You are silent, it is because You are aligning the right moment, the right people, and the right resources. Teach him to wait with patience instead of panic.

Remind him that seeking wise counsel is strength, not weakness. Surround him with mentors, advisors, and brothers who confirm what You have already whispered to his heart.

And when the road feels unclear, remind him he is not lost, he is being led. You know exactly where he is and exactly where You are taking him next.

Thank You, God, for being his compass, his guide, and the light on his path.
Amen.

Scripture Reading:

"Trust in the Lord with all your heart and lean not on your own understanding; in all your ways submit to him, and he will make your paths straight." — Proverbs 3:5–6 (NIV)

Today's Challenge:

Identify one area where you need direction today. Pray: "God, I trust You. Lead me in the way I should go." Spend five minutes in silence listening for His guidance, then write what you hear.

Daily Reminder Quote:

"When you do not know what to do next, trust the One who sees the end from the beginning." — *Ebony N. Mayo*

Journal Space:

(Write about where you feel directionless and what clarity you are asking God for in this season.)

_____

_____

_____

_____

_____

_____

_____

_____

_____

_____

_____

_____

_____

_____

JOY

(Finding Strength Beyond Happiness)

Reflection Question:

Do you feel true joy right now, or have you settled for temporary happiness? What would it look like to live with unshakeable joy, regardless of circumstances?

DEAR GOD, THANK YOU FOR THIS AMAZING MAN:

God, today I pray for joy to rise up in this man's life. Not fleeting happiness that shifts with circumstances, but deep, unshakable joy that comes only from You.

You see the heaviness he carries. The responsibilities that weigh on his shoulders. The silent frustrations and disappointments that have tried to steal his smile. The moments when he laughs in public, but feels numb in private.

God, restore his joy today. Help him to see that *the joy of the Lord is his strength.* This joy is not the same as worldly happiness that depends on external factors. Instead, it is a deep, unshakable inner strength that comes from Your presence and love. Remind him that joy is a gift from You, a gift that transforms, sustains, and empowers him to endure hardships and to walk in faith even when the path is hard.

Remove anything that drains his joy: toxic thoughts, negative environments, unforgiveness, bitterness, fear of the future, and regret of the past.

Fill him with joy that carries him through storms. Joy that lights up his home, his work, and his relationships. Joy that makes him laugh again, hope again, and dream again. Let his joy be contagious, shifting the atmosphere everywhere he goes.

And God, remind him that joy is not just a feeling, it is a weapon. Joy pushes back the darkness. Joy confuses the enemy. Joy declares that no matter what life throws at him, he still wins because You are with him. When fear rises, let joy fight for him. When discouragement whispers, let joy silence it. When hopelessness tries to creep in, let joy drive it out.

God, help him to choose joy daily. To notice blessings in the small moments. To be present with the people who love him. To celebrate progress even when the finish line feels far away.

Thank You for being the well that never runs dry. When life drains him, refill him with joy that can not be shaken by loss, fear, or failure. Let tomorrow meet him with fresh strength, new perspective, and a renewed heart anchored in joy.
Amen.

Scripture Reading:

"Do not grieve, for the joy of the Lord is your strength." — Nehemiah 8:10 (NIV)

Today's Challenge:

Write down three things you are grateful for today. Pray: "God, fill me with Your joy that gives me strength beyond my circumstances." Do one thing today that brings you genuine joy, music, laughter, conversation, creativity, or rest.

Daily Reminder Quote:

"Joy is more than a feeling; it is a strength, a gift, and a weapon. Walk in it daily." — Ebony N. Mayo

Journal Space:

(Write about where you have lost joy and what you believe God wants to restore in your spirit today.)

_____

_____

_____

_____

_____

_____

_____

_____

_____

_____

_____

_____

_____

DISCIPLINE

(Choosing What You Want Most
Over What You Want Now)

Reflection Question:

Where in your life do you lack discipline right now? What would change if you became more consistent and committed in that area?

DEAR GOD, THANK YOU FOR THIS AMAZING MAN:

God, today I pray for discipline in this man's life. You see where he struggles to stay consistent. You see the habits that keep him stuck and the excuses that hold him back from becoming the man You created him to be.

God, give him supernatural discipline today. Discipline to wake up when his alarm goes off. Discipline to focus on what matters instead of wasting time on distractions that do not move him forward. Discipline to close the apps, turn off the TV, and stop pouring energy into things that do not build his future. Discipline to care for his health, to eat what fuels him, to move his body, to rest when needed. Discipline to manage his money with wisdom instead of chasing impulse desires. Discipline to guard his eyes, his ears, and his heart from habits that steal his strength and poison his spirit.

God, help him to see that discipline is not punishment, it is protection. It is freedom. It is becoming a man who is trusted because he is consistent. It is building the life You have called him to live, brick by brick, day by day.

Remove laziness, procrastination, and excuses from his mindset. Replace them with focus, intentionality, and commitment. Strengthen his will when motivation fades. Remind him that real discipline is not about perfection, it is about progress. Small, consistent steps daily that lead to big victories long-term.

God, let him be disciplined in his relationships choosing faithfulness, patience, and love even when it is hard. Let him be disciplined in his emotions, not lashing out in anger, not shutting down, but showing up with wisdom and self-control. Let him be disciplined in his faith praying, studying, and staying rooted in You, even when it feels easier to drift.

Thank You, God, for loving him enough to correct and sharpen him. Help him to embrace discipline not as a burden, but as a gift that unlocks purpose, power, and legacy.
Amen.

Scripture Reading:

"No discipline seems pleasant at the time, but painful. Later on, however, it produces a harvest of righteousness and peace for those who have been trained by it." — Hebrews 12:11 (NIV)

Today's Challenge:

Identify one area where you have been wasting time. Pray: "God, give me the strength to be disciplined and consistent today." Replace that distraction with one intentional step toward your goals.

Daily Reminder Quote:

"Discipline is the bridge between potential and legacy. Build it daily." — Ebony N. Mayo

Journal Space:

(Write about where you lack discipline, why it has been hard, and
what your life would look like if you became consistent in that area.)

_____

_____

_____

_____

_____

_____

_____

_____

_____

_____

_____

_____

_____

_____

TRUST

(Letting Go of Control and Learning to Trust Again)

Reflection Question:

Where in your life are you struggling to trust God, yourself, or others? What would it look like to release fear and walk in trust again?

DEAR GOD, THANK YOU FOR THIS AMAZING MAN:

*G*od, today I pray for this man's trust. Not just his trust in You, but his ability to trust period.

You see where his faith feels shaky. Where fear whispers that he is alone. Where anxiety pushes him to control what was never his to carry. God, remind him that You are trustworthy that You have never failed him and You will not start now.

But God, I also pray for his trust in life, in people, and in himself. Heal the parts of him that were broken when someone betrayed his trust. The places where words cut deep. The relationships where loyalty was shattered. The seasons where he let himself down and began to believe he could not be trusted with his own choices.

God, restore his ability to trust love again. If he has been hurt by a partner, remind him that not all love ends in pain. If he has been guarded because of heartbreak, disappointment, or betrayal, show him that real, genuine, lasting love still exists. Remind him that he is worthy of being chosen, honored, and cherished without having to perform, prove, or pretend. Prepare his heart for the right love, and prepare him to give love fully without fear of rejection.

Teach him to trust himself again, his instincts, his gifts, his discernment. Show him that just because he made mistakes in the past does not mean he is destined to repeat them. Help him believe in his own growth, his own wisdom, and the new man You are shaping him into.

And God, restore his trust in brotherhood and friendship. If he has been let down by friends who walked away, betrayed by those he counted on, or isolated because he thought he had to carry it all alone, heal those wounds. Surround him with men of character, loyalty, and faith who will sharpen him, lift him, and cover him in prayer. Help him see that he does not have to do life by himself and that safe, genuine brotherhood is still possible.

And most of all, God, help him to trust the process. To know that even when he cannot see the full picture, You are painting something greater. Replace his worry with worship, his doubt with confidence, and his fear with faith. Let trust become his posture in You, in himself, in love, and in the people You have assigned to walk with him.

Thank You, God, for being his Provider, Healer, Redeemer, and Safe Place. Thank You for teaching him that trust is strength, not weakness. Help him to live today with an open heart not guarded by fear, but grounded in faith.
Amen.

Scripture Reading:

"Trust in the Lord with all your heart and lean not on your own understanding; in all your ways submit to him, and he will make your paths straight." — Proverbs 3:5–6 (NIV)

Today's Challenge:

Identify one area where you have struggled to trust whether in God, yourself, love, or others. Pray: "God, help me release fear and rebuild trust in this area of my life." Take one small step today that reflects trust instead of self-protection.

Daily Reminder Quote:

"Trust is the bridge between fear and freedom; it heals your faith, your relationships, and your future." — *Ebony N. Mayo*

Journal Space:

(Write about where trust has been broken in your life and what it would look like to rebuild it with God's help.)

_____

_____

_____

_____

_____

_____

_____

_____

_____

_____

_____

_____

_____

_____

LEGACY

(Leaving a Mark That Outlives You)

Reflection Question:

What legacy are you building right now? If your life ended today, what would people say you stood for?

DEAR GOD, THANK YOU FOR THIS AMAZING MAN:

*G*od, today I pray about this man's legacy. Thank You that You created him with purpose, not just to live for today, but to build something that outlives him.

Remind him that legacy is not optional. He is leaving one, whether he chooses it intentionally or not. Help him to realize that every word he speaks, every decision he makes, every seed he sows is shaping the story his children, his family, and his community will tell about him.

God, help him to live with the weight and the wonder of legacy in mind. To know that if he does not live in his purpose, his legacy will be incomplete. That if he drifts without direction, he risks passing down confusion instead of clarity, brokenness instead of blessing. Teach him that his obedience to purpose is not just about him, but that it affects his children, his children's children, and generations yet to be born.

God, give him wisdom to build a kingdom legacy not just wealth that fades, but values that last. A legacy of integrity. A legacy of faith. A legacy of strength, love, and wisdom that will ripple far beyond his lifetime.

Remind him of this truth: *When a man does not live his purpose, his children inherit his silence instead of his wisdom. His family inherits his pain instead of his peace. His community inherits his absence instead of his presence.* But when he chooses purpose, he plants seeds of hope, courage, and victory that will bloom for generations.

God, let him build differently. Let him live intentionally. Let him choose faithfulness over comfort, so his children inherit courage instead of fear. Let him choose discipline over recklessness, so his family inherits stability instead of struggle. Let him choose purpose over distraction, so the story of his life points back to You.

And God, if he feels like his past has damaged his legacy, redeem it. Rewrite his story. Remind him it is never too late to shift the narrative and leave behind something greater than what he received.

Thank You, God, that when he walks in purpose, he also walks in legacy. That his name will carry weight not because of what he had, but because of how he lived. Help him to finish strong and to leave a legacy that declares: "Here stood a man of God. A man of character. A man of love. A man who made his life count."
Amen.

Scripture Reading:

"A good man leaves an inheritance to his children's children" — Proverbs 13:22 (NKJV)

Today's Challenge:

Write down the kind of legacy you want to leave behind. Pray: "God, help me to live with legacy in mind, and let my purpose shape generations to come." Take one intentional action today that aligns with the story you want your life to tell.

Daily Reminder Quote:

"Legacy is not what you leave for people, it is what you leave in them. Live with purpose, so your story outlives you." — *Ebony N. Mayo*

Journal Space:

(Write about the legacy you are building now and what needs to shift
to align with the vision God has for you.)

_____

_____

_____

_____

_____

_____

_____

_____

_____

_____

_____

_____

_____

_____

FATHERHOOD

(Raising Kings, Building Legacy)

Reflection Question:

How are you showing up as a father today not just in provision, but in presence, patience, and love?

DEAR GOD, THANK YOU FOR THIS AMAZING MAN:

*G*od, today I pray for this man as a father. You see his heart, the weight he carries to protect, provide, and guide his children. You see the silent pressure he feels to get it all right, even when he is still healing from the places where his own father may have fallen short.

God, strengthen him to show up with patience when he feels stretched thin. Remind him that fatherhood is not about perfection it is about presence. Help him to understand that his children need his love more than they need his money, his attention more than his approval, and his time more than his titles.

God, I pray especially for the fathers who work so much that they miss the small moments, the laughter at dinner tables, the bedtime stories, the questions that go unanswered. Help them to realize that while money provides, time shapes. Let them know that a paycheck can cover expenses, but presence covers the soul. Remind them that children will not always remember what was bought, but they will always remember who showed up. Teach him to create balance, to prioritize what cannot be replaced, and to guard his time with his children like the treasure it is.

God, I lift up fathers who long to be with their children, but do not have the opportunity. Whether because of distance, divorce, broken relationships, court systems, or circumstances beyond their control, comfort their hearts. Protect their children when they cannot be there. Remind them that their prayers still cover their sons and daughters, even from afar. Encourage them to keep showing love in the ways they can and to never give up hope for restoration and reconnection.

And God, I pray for the men who grew up fatherless. For the boys who became men without a guide, a role model, or a covering. Heal the wounds left by absence. Remind them that even without a father's example, they are not disqualified from being great fathers themselves. Show them that they are breaking cycles, rewriting stories, and becoming the men their children will proudly look up to.

God, I also lift up the full-time fathers, the ones who do it all by themselves, the ones no one talks about. The men who work all day, cook, clean, show up at games, help with homework, pray at night, and give every ounce of themselves to their children 24 hours a day. God, strengthen them when they feel unseen or unappreciated. Remind them that You see their sacrifice. Remind them that their children see their love. And remind them that their labor is not in vain, because they are raising a legacy with every meal cooked, every ride given, every tear wiped, and every prayer whispered.

God, heal him from the mistakes of yesterday. Release him from guilt if he was not always there before. Show him that every new day is another chance to love better, lead better, and model what a true man of God looks like.

Protect his children keep them safe, healthy, and on the path of purpose. Let his voice be the one that affirms them when the world tries to tear them down. Let his example be the blueprint they remember long after they are grown.

And if he does not yet have children but desires to, prepare him now. Build him into the man, the partner, and the leader who will raise sons into kings and daughters into queens.

Thank You, God, for fathers who love, protect, and guide. Thank You for trusting him with the sacred role of fatherhood. May he leave a legacy that outlives him, written not just in words, but in the lives of the children he is raising.
Amen.

Scripture Reading:

"Fathers, do not provoke your children to anger, but bring them up in the discipline and instruction of the Lord." — Ephesians 6:4 (ESV)

Today's Challenge:

Take one intentional step today to show love to your children (or the children you influence). Call them, hug them, encourage them, or pray over them.

Daily Reminder Quote:

"Fatherhood is not just about raising children, it is about raising Kings and Queens, building legacy, and shaping the future." — Ebony N. Mayo

Journal Space:

(Write about what fatherhood means to you, the father you want to be, and how you can be more present and intentional. If you are separated from your children, write a prayer for them here.)

_____

_____

_____

_____

_____

_____

_____

_____

_____

_____

_____

_____

_____

INTIMACY WITH GOD

(*Moving From Religion to Relationship*)

Reflection Question:

Do you feel truly close to God or has your relationship with Him felt distant, routine, or surface-level? What would intimacy with God look like for you personally?

DEAR GOD, THANK YOU FOR THIS AMAZING MAN:

*G*od, today I pray for this man's intimacy with You. Not just knowledge about You, not just religion, not just routine but real, living relationship. A closeness that feels like breath, like heartbeat, like home.

God, remove the lies that tell him he has to perform to earn Your love. Remind him that You are not looking for perfection, You are looking for presence. That intimacy begins with honesty, his raw thoughts, his unspoken fears, his hidden questions.

Break down every barrier that has stood between him and You. The shame that tells him he is too unworthy. The guilt that whispers he has made too many mistakes. The busyness that convinces him he does not have time. The distractions, stress, endless obligations that pull him away before he can even pause. God, silence those lies and teach him that You are not asking for his performance, You are asking for his presence.

If he has been hurt by people proclaiming Your Name, remind him not to confuse Your perfection with human imperfection. Show him that his faith is not about flawed people, but about a flawless God. Heal the sting of those wounds and give him the strength to forgive those who misrepresented You, so their actions do not keep him from Your presence.

Heal the places where father wounds, mother scars, rejection, or betrayal made it hard for him to trust closeness. Show him that You are not like those who failed him. You are the Father who never leaves. The Friend who never betrays. The God who never stops pursuing him.

Teach him to invite You into every space not just Sunday mornings, but his work, his workouts, his finances, his relationships, his parenting, his private thoughts. Let intimacy with You be his daily rhythm, not just a moment.

God, help him to hear Your voice with clarity. To recognize Your whispers over the noise. To sense Your guidance in his decisions. To walk so closely with You that others can see Your reflection in his life.

Thank You, God, that intimacy with You produces peace, strength, wisdom, and joy. Thank You that You are not a distant God You are Emmanuel, God with us. With him. Right now.

Draw him in, God. Closer than he has ever been. Let him know he is not just a servant or soldier, but a son who can crawl into his Father's arms and rest.
Amen.

Scripture Reading:

"Draw near to God, and he will draw near to you." — James 4:8 (ESV)

Today's Challenge:

Spend 10 minutes today with God, no requests, no distractions, no agenda. Just His presence and stillness.

Daily Reminder Quote:

"Intimacy with God is not about religion, it is about relationship. Do not confuse God's perfection with people's imperfection. God does not just want your time, God wants your heart." — *Ebony N. Mayo*

Journal Space:

(Write about what intimacy with God would look like for you. Where have you felt distant, and what would help you draw closer?)

_____

_____

_____

_____

_____

_____

_____

_____

_____

_____

_____

_____

_____

_____

_____

IDENTITY

(Who You Are Beyond Titles and Roles)

Reflection Question:

Who are you when you strip away your job, your money, your status, or your mistakes? Do you know who you truly are?

DEAR GOD, THANK YOU FOR THIS AMAZING MAN:

*G*od, today I pray for this man's identity. Remind him that he is more than his job title, his paycheck, or the roles he plays. He is more than what he produces, more than the mistakes he has made, and more than the opinions others have spoken over him.

God, silence the lies that told him he was "not enough." Cancel the labels people placed on him when he was young the names, the insults, the doubts, the limitations. Heal the wounds from parents, teachers, partners, or friends who made him feel small, unseen, or unworthy.

God, remind him that his identity is secure in You. That he is Your son. That he is chosen, loved, forgiven, redeemed, and called. That he does not have to perform to be worthy. He does not have to prove to be valuable. He does not have to compare to measure up.

Help him to stop defining himself by what he does or what he has and to start defining himself by who You say he is. Give him confidence to walk boldly in his true identity: a man of strength, vision, honor, and purpose.

And when insecurity tries to creep back in, whisper to his spirit: "You are mine. You are loved. You are enough."

Thank You, God, for creating him in Your image. Help him to walk in the truth of who he really is, not a broken version of himself, but the masterpiece You designed.
Amen.

Scripture Reading:

"But you are a chosen people, a royal priesthood, a holy nation, God's special possession…" — 1 Peter 2:9 (NIV)

Today's Challenge:

Write down three truths about who you are in God beyond your job, your money, or what others have said. Say them out loud today.

Daily Reminder Quote:

"Your identity is not in what you have done or what you have; it is in who God says. You are chosen, loved, and enough." — Ebony N. Mayo

Journal Space:

(Reflect on who you have believed you were vs. who God says you are.)

_____

_____

_____

_____

_____

_____

_____

_____

_____

_____

_____

_____

_____

_____

_____

DECLARATION FOR KINGS

Congratulations, King. You have taken intentional time to pause, pray, and reflect. That alone proves your strength and commitment to becoming the man God created you to be.

You made it. Not by perfection, but by presence. Not by rushing, but by showing up. Every prayer, every journal moment, every pause to reflect, it all mattered.

If you are reading this, know this: **I am proud of you and your journey.**

This devotional was never just about words on a page. It was about you choosing to heal, to grow, and to stand in your truth. It was about you realizing that even the strongest man deserves rest, love, and grace.

You are not the same man who started this journey. You are more aware. More grounded. More connected to God, yourself, and your purpose.

But this is not the end, it is the beginning of a new chapter.

Your Call to Action Is Simple:

- Keep praying.
- Keep journaling.
- Keep becoming.
- Keep walking in truth, power, and peace.
- And most importantly, bring another brother with you. Uplift someone else, share what you have gained, and create the kind of community that makes all of us stronger.

King, you have done something many men will never do. You slowed down long enough to hear God, to hear yourself, and to heal.

Now go forward boldly. Live this. Walk this. Be this. And shine your light for the world to see.

From This Day Forward, Declare These Truths Over Your Life:

- I am loved by God, fully and completely.
- I am worthy of peace, success, and joy.
- I release fear, doubt, and comparison.
- I embrace discipline, gratitude, and trust.
- I am a protector, provider, and builder of legacy.
- I set boundaries that honor my worth.
- I am surrounded by community and covered by blessings.
- I am a King walking in truth, power, and purpose.
- I am proud of myself and the journey I am on.
- I am becoming greater every day.

Remember:

King, keep praying. Keep growing. Keep shining. Keep becoming.
This is not the end, it is the continuation of your greatness.
Blessings, love, and light, **Ebony N. Mayo**
For more information visit www.ebonynmayo.com
Email: info@ebonynmayo.com

Scan my QR code above
or visit www.ebonynmayo.com
or email us at info@ebonynmayo.com